A Teenage War

War

Fighting Lust, Lies, Depression, And Darkness In A Generation That Forgot Who They Are

Caleb A. Calloway

MISSIONAL
PUBLISHING

All scripture quoted is from New International Version, Zondervan Publishing unless otherwise noted.

ISBN: 978-0-9890950-4-4

1. Christian life. 2. God (Christianity). 3. Self help techniques

MISSIONAL
PUBLISHING

Dedication

I want to dedicate this book to my aunt Flossie. She taught everyone how to love hard and to always be joyful of the situation.

I also want to dedicate this to all of those who have struggled with these issues addressed in this book as well as any body who is struggling right now, remember **God is with us!**

Introduction

A Broken Generation, A Mighty God

They say this is the most connected generation in history, but it might also be the loneliest.

We have access to everything, but connection to nothing. Endless scrolls of people's lives, AI that can answer any question, instant dopamine hits from likes, shares, and emojis even. But in the middle of all that noise, we've lost our silence. Our minds have become like battlefields, filled with attacks from the enemy. Our hearts which were once sensitive and full of wonder and joy have been hijacked by screens, shame, and secrets we're too afraid to share.

I'm not writing this book to someone who's got it all together, because I've not got it all figured out. I'm a fifteen-year-old boy, soon to be sixteen from a small town in NE Ohio, trying to spread my testimony and the great word of GOD! My great Heavenly Father. I'm writing this because I've been there. I've been up at 2:00 am staring at the ceiling asking God why I feel so numb. I've lied to people's faces while hiding sin in my heart. I've gone to school acting like everything was fine while last night I sat with a razor blade on my wrists begging God to just let me end it.

This book isn't a sermon. It's a rescue rope. And I hope you hang onto this rope and let the journey of crawling up to the peace God brings. This book is the result of of my personal life experience and is pulled from hundreds of pages of personal Bible study notes, and many, many sermon notes from several pastors. As a disclaimer, I utilized artificial intelligence as a tool to help me pull it all together into this book.

We are living in a time when the world is pulling harder than ever on the minds and hearts of young people. Lust is no longer something whispered about, its marketed and fueled in the schools. Trust me I know, I have struggled with lust since I was 9, just waiting for one day it to take over my life and me never tell a single person because it is a silent sin, a sin that would be shunned in the generation we live in. Addiction isn't something rare, its designed into every app and social platform. And pushed upon us as young teens as a norm, everyone thinks hitting a vape, or drinking alcohol is the cool thing to do. That's not what God has said though. Depression isn't just a phase; it's a weight that crushes more teens now than ever before. Suicide is the **third** leading cause of death for ages 10-24 according to the Center for Disease Control. More teenagers and young adults die from suicide than from cancer, heart diseases, AIDS, birth defects, strokes, pneumonia, the flu, and chronic lung disease **COMBINED.** Each day in the USA there is an average of over 3,703 attempts by students in grades 9-12. And the sad thing is most teenagers give some sort of sign of the intent. 4 out of 5 individuals considering suicide give some sign of their intentions either verbally or behaviorally (The Parent Resource Program). And while we live in this generation that tells people to "be yourself", the world hands you a dozen broken versions of who that "self" is supposed to be.

Schools, instead of being a safe place to grow, have become spiritual battlegrounds. Young women wearing revealing clothes, people doing drugs in the bathroom, lying, fights, false friends (I know my first taste of lust came from a fourth-grade classroom, my friend who will not be named for privacy, showed me a website that as a Christian I knew I shouldn't be looking at. Then end of 5th grade came when I really was able to break free from that warfare, and it was only by the deep study of God's word and love that I could feel free). They don't just leave God out; they push Him out. Purity is mocked. Holiness is seen as not cool or outdated. The truth we learn in church and in His word is now considered "offensive", and confusion is celebrated. Teachers preach tolerance and numbness to this world's issues, and they forget the truth. And students, barely old enough to understand what's happening inside of them, are told to define their whole identity which should be in Jesus's Holy name, to be apart from their Creator.

But here's the good news: **God isn't afraid of this generations mess. He actually loves cleaning us up, remember He sent His son to die for our MESS!**

The Bible is not just some old, irrelevant to this time book. It's a weapon, map, a voice calling out in the middle of the chaos that us as Christians use. And Jesus? He's not distant. He's not to holy to touch your pain. He meets you right where you are, scrolling alone at night, overwhelmed by guilt, trying to keep the mask on around your "friends" or hiding the scars nobody knows about.

This book is a wakeup call. Not just to see the lies you've been sold, but to know that **FREEDOM IS POSSIBLE.** You don't have to be addicted. You don't have to feel loved or defined by lust. You don't have to live depressed, hopeless, or confused of what's next, of who's going to hurt me next or leave me next, or what happens if they come back.

You were made for more.

So, if you're tired of *faking it*, tired of *feeling empty,* tired of scrolling through *false answers,* this book... no, this guide is for you. We're going to talk about some REAL struggles, not sugarcoat them because this world needs reassurance that they are not alone in these hard situations. We are going to expose the systems that shape your mind when no one's paying attention. And most of all, we're going to talk about the only one who can truly make you whole again. **Jesus Christ.**

You weren't born into peace. You were born into a war, constantly fighting against the enemy, but Jesus takes that fight off your hands on the cross.

Maybe no one ever told you that. Maybe you thought life was just about growing up, getting good grades, finding someone to love, chasing a career, and being "happy". But there's a war going on, a war for your souls, your mind, your future. And the enemy isn't playing fair.

He starts early. He whispers lies while you're still young. He uses subtle things such as...

- TikTok's
- Music
- Friends
- Education Systems

These things not always evil on the surface, but dangerous when you let your guard down. He doesn't come with horns and a pitchfork banging at your door. He comes through the glow of your phone screen, the trauma you never healed from, the need for love that gets twisted into lust. And he's patient. He knows if he can distract you, addict you, or shame you when you're young, he can stunt your spiritual and emotional growth for years... sometimes your whole life.

Satan doesn't need to turn you into a devil worshipper. he just needs to keep you numb, busy and blind.

But here's what I believe: **God is raising up a remnant, you are not alone.**

You might feel weak right now. You might feel like you're too far gone, that no one ever could love you. Maybe you've already made mistakes you don't want to admit. But God specializes in using broken people to do powerful things. When Jesus walked this earth, He didn't pick the religious elite, he picked the messy, the angry, the rejected, the sinful and he turned them into disciples. Examples are...

Noah was a drunk. Abraham was too old. Isaac was a day dreamer and wanderer. Jacob was a liar. Leah was ugly. Moses was a murderer. Gideon was afraid. Samson was a "flirt". Rahab was a prostitute. David was an adulterer and murderer. Elijah was suicidal. Isaiah preached naked. Jonah ran away from God. John the Baptist ate bugs. Peter denied Jesus not just once, twice, but three times! The disciples fell asleep while Jesus was praying. God doesn't care what you've done. He always loves you.

He's not looking for perfect. He's looking for willing.

This generation doesn't need more "nice" Christians. It needs warriors. Young people with a backbone. Teens who aren't afraid to pray out loud, to delete things that are killing them too fast and fight for purity, to be different even when it costs them everything they may want or have.

There is no revival without repentance.

God's not calling you to church attendance alone. He's calling you to lay down your idols (lust, pride, comfort, addiction) and to walk in real power, which only can come from *Him*. This book may hit some soft spots and will hit hard because the world is hitting you even harder. But every page you read is a step towards freedom. Not the fake kind the world offers. Not temporary relief. But healing. Restoration. Purpose. Truth.

This isn't just any book... This is a call to step out of the numbness and into the fire of God. And it's a fire that doesn't burn you, it purifies you.

How to Read This Book

- **Be honest with yourself.** Don't skim through just to finish. Sit with what makes you uncomfortable.

- **Pray as you read.** Even if it's simple. "God, help me hear what you want to say to me, for I am trying to become quieter and live a quieter life"

- **Journal your thoughts.** What's hitting you? What's God saying? What's hard to let go of?

- **Don't give up.** If something convicts you, that's grace. Stay with it. Wrestle. God meets you in the struggle.

- **Talk to someone.** I know it's hard, it is, trust me I get it. It's the fear of that person being ashamed of you or you getting in trouble. But it is the only way to true revival and loss of that sin. Share with a mentor, youth pastor, or parent you trust. I recommend the first two.

By the time you finish this book, I pray you're not just "inspired", I pray you're transformed.

Because you enter both into war. But with Jesus, **you were also born to win!**

Contents

Chapter 1: The Seeds of Lust

L ust rarely starts with a scream. It starts with a whisper.

"But I tell you, everyone who looks at women lustfully has already committed adultery with her in his heart". Matthew 5:28 (CSB)

A glance. A thought. A scroll. A scene you weren't even looking for plants something in your mind, a burning desire for you just viewed. Something you can't unsee. That seed sits there, and unless it's ripped out early, it grows. It grows into habits then into shame, then into a whole lifestyle that you never meant to build.

Most people won't talk about it, but we need to. Lust is one of the most accepted sins in our culture and one of the most destructive. We have kids in high school having sex with someone they will break up with in two months. Or kids sending nude pictures to each other that if they send it to the wrong person, it will get taken and shown to a group of people then eventually the whole school knows what the body that God made beautiful or handsome looks like.

> Lust hides under the surface like a silent killer. It doesn't just affect your actions, it rewires your brain, damages your ability to love, and distances yourself from God.

Let's be clear: lust is not attraction. God made us to see beauty. He made us to love. But sin takes that design and twists it. Lust turns people into objects. It reduces intimacy into a transaction. It chokes out real love and replaces it with a craving. That if you don't fill it, you go searching for other people, or things to fill it. That's why we have the hook-up culture today.

And for many of us, it started young. Maybe you found porn by accident when you were nine years old. Maybe a friend showed you something "funny" that turned into a habit such as it happened to me. Maybe you got used to thirst traps on social media and didn't even realize that your mind was getting trained and taught to lust constantly.

It's not just what you do, it's how you start seeing people. People's sons and daughters.

You stop seeing people as made in Gods image and start seeing them as something to consume and to feel pleasure from. And sometimes it's not even a consensual taste, your brain gets so twisted that you start forcing people to do it and to send you those pictures, and to touch you there. Maybe it's because someone when you were young touched you like that without your consent, or made you do those things to them, and told you that if you would tell anyone you would be the person at fault. And now you feel as if that's the only way you can feel "love" even though that's not what love is.

Here's the thing: lust doesn't always feel evil when it begins. Sometimes it feels exciting. Curiosity mixed with desire. Something new. Something forbidden. It makes your heart race and your thoughts spin, but no one knows it happened. You bury it. You tell yourself, "I'll stop after this time" or "It's not really that bad"

That's how the trap is set

Lust thrives in silence. It feeds on secrecy. It grows stronger every time you pretend it's not there. The more you hide it, the more it hides in you, until it's no longer as thought but a habit, and no longer a habit but an identity when that identity should be a follower of Jesus Christ.

Before you know it, it's shaping how you see the world. You walk into school, and size people up not by who they are, but how attractive they are. You scroll through social media looking for just enough skin to stir something, but not enough to feel guilty. You find yourself watching people, not as souls but their bodies. You compare, you fantasize, and you feel hollow afterwards.

It's no longer a whisper but a voice, and it says things like

- "You'll never stop"

- "Everyone does it"

- "You're too far gone now"

- "God wouldn't want someone like you"

But I'm here today to tell you that voice is a liar.
And that voice is not from God.

What Lust Really Is
Lust is not just a desire, it's a distortion.

God created desire. God created sex. God created romance. But sin twists these beautiful things and offers us counterfeits. Cheap versions. Imitations that don't satisfy.

Lust gives you the shell of love without the substance. It's fast, but its shallow. It's intense, but its hollow. It's tempting but never fulfills.

And worst of all, it doesn't stay small. Lust never stops asking for more.

What began with a glance becomes a video. What began with a fantasy becomes an action. What began with one secret becomes a web of lies, shame, and habits that eat away your spirit.

Many teens walk into this trap without ever realizing what's happening. The enemy doesn't need to destroy you in one moment, he just needs you distracted, addicted and ashamed long enough to keep you from walking into your **calling.** If Satan can take your eyes, he'll start taking your heart.

"*The eye is the lamp of the body. If your eyes are healthy, your whole body will be full of light*" Matthew 6:22

Lust clouds that lamp. It fogs your spiritual vision. You stop seeing people as image bearers of God and start seeing them as images to use. You stop pursuing relationships with depth and settle for fantasies with no commitment. You start seeking God and start hiding from Him.

Sadly, most people will start to believe that this is just who you are now.

But let me be real with you: Lust may have started in your life, but here's the good news it doesn't have to stay.

You can stop watering that seed.

You can dig it up, burn it at the altar. Let God rip it out, even If it hurts.

Because what God wants to grow in your life is far more powerful than the counterfeit you're chasing. He doesn't want to shame you; He wants to free you.

The Digital Playground of Sin

The enemy doesn't need to drag you into a strip club, he just needs you to unlock your phone.

What used to take effort, sneaking a magazine, going to sketchy websites, is now available with one tap. That's the sad part and reality of the world I personally was born into and that many teenagers as myself have fallen a victim of. You don't even have to search for sin anymore. It comes looking for you. It finds you through ads, explore pages, "For You" algorithms, and pop-up disguised as jokes or trends.

What used to be hidden in back alleys, now lives in your back pocket.

This generation didn't just grow up with phones, we were basically raised by them. And it's not even out faults, we weren't the ones to create them. Raised by screens that constantly flash bodies, temptation, and content made to hook your attention and hijack your heart. You don't even notice it at first. That's what makes it so dangerous. It's not always full-blown porn at first. Sometimes it's the subtle stuff:

-The dance challenge with just a little too much skin

-The "harmless" video that lingers a little too long

-The influencer who posts for likes but steals your purity in the process

These moments train your mind. They reshape your brain. And over time, they normalize lust. What should make you uncomfortable begins to feel "Normal". What once made your heart race now leaves you numb, but still reaching for more.

Because this is what this playground to the devil is and was designed to do.

The Trap is Designed

Here is something you need to understand: you're not weak for falling into temptation, you were targeted from the time you were born.

Billions of dollars are spent designing apps that study your behavior. They track what makes you pause. They log what you click. They learn your temptations better than you do, and then they feed it back to you, a little more each time.

You're not just using technology, it's using you.

And for many the result is a full-blown addiction before age 15.

Here's how the cycle goes:

- **You get curious**- A moment of boredom turns into a search.

- **You get excited**- Dopamine rush. You feel powerful. In control.

- **You finish**- Guilt kicks in. You promise yourself it's the last time.

- **You go numb**- Conviction fades. Temptation returns.

- **Repeat**- Again. And again. And again

Before long, your phone is no longer a tool. It's a leash.

Why Porn and Lust Are So Dangerous

Porn doesn't just stain your screen. It stains your soul. Every time you engage with lust in secret, it does something spiritual. It trains your heart to choose temporary satisfaction over eternal purpose. It numbs your ability to love deeply. And worst of all... it disconnects you from the voice of God.

You don't lose your salvation every time you fall, but you lose clarity. You stop hearing Gods voice clearly. You stop wanting to pray. You feel fake in worship. You pull away from people who could help. And you start to believe the lie: "This is just who I am"

Let me tell you something the devil doesn't what you to hear:

YOUR NOT ADDICTED. YOUR UNDER ATTACK.

And what's been learned can be unlearned. What's broken, can be fixed. What's been corrupted can be made clean. By GOD.

You Were Made for More

God didn't design you to live in chains. He didn't create your body or your mind to be trapped in a screen, chasing shadows and false depiction of real love.

You were made for wholeness. For joy. For freedom that doesn't fade the second the screen goes black. The playground the world offers is fake. The love it mimics is counterfeit. But the joy of God is real. It's deep. It's lasting. And it's yours, if you lay down your phone enough to pick up your cross.

"Blessed are the pure in heart, for they will see God" Matthew 5:8

Don't you want that? Don't you want to see God again, to feel Him, to hear His voice again? It starts with repentance. It starts with deleting what's killing you. It starts with giving up the fake so you can receive the real.

And the Good news?

It's not too late.

Not even close.

What Lust Really Steals

The world doesn't show you the aftermath. It shows you the bait but hides the trap. It makes lust look glamorous but doesn't show you the weight of what it takes from you. Lust isn't harmless. It isn't neutral. It's slow, silent thief, and here's what it steals.

1. Your Mind

Lust poisons how you think. It clouds your judgement. It rewires your brain to crave short-term pleasure, and makes discipline feel like torture. It makes school harder. Focus harder. Reading the Bible harder. Why?

Because your brain has been trained to expect constant hits of dopamine, those instant rewards that come with every image, every click, every fantasy. We enjoy the hits of dopamine that began at an early age with praise from parents, family, teachers, friends, and coaches. Nothing wrong with those types of praise, but we enjoy it and thrive for it.

You might start forgetting how to focus on class, how to carry deep conversations, or even how to be alone with your thoughts that aren't unclean. Worst of all it messed with your imagination. Instead of dreaming about your future, your calling, or your purpose, you start daydreaming about images that don't even know your name or love you back.

2. Your Relationships

Lust makes you selfish. It teaches you to take, not to give. To expect intimacy without sacrifice. To want connection without commitment. Before long, your view of people changes. You're not looking at hearts, you're scanning bodies. You're not getting to know someone; you're evaluating them for how well they fit your fantasy. And when you try to form a real relationship, it's hard. You get bored quickly. You feel frustrated quickly. You feel frustrated easily. You can't separate love from lust, so you either chase intensity or avoid commitment altogether.

Even friendships start to suffer. You isolate yourself. You lie. You avoid eye contact. You feel like a fake around people who love God, and instead of running to them, you run from them. Why? Because lust doesn't just affect how you treat others. It affects how you see yourself

3. Your Identity

Lust builds shame. And shame builds a false identity.

You start thinking:

"I'm dirty"

"I'm addicted"

"I'm a fake Christian"

"I'll never be free"

But hear me, those lies are not who you are. They are who the enemy wants you to believe you are, because as long as you believe that you'll stay in bondage. The longer you live in lust, the more you forget what it felt like to be clean. To walk in freedom. To have a clear conscience. You get so used to hiding your sin, you forget what it feels like to walk in the light. But God has never forgot who you are. He never stopped seeing the real you. Even when covered in sin. He saw a son. A daughter. A warrior. A child worth dying for.

4. Your Purpose

You were made for something eternal. Lust tries to convince you your only goal is pleasure, but God has called you to impact lives. To build families. To disciple friends. To use your gifts for something eternal. But lust keeps you small. Distracted. Numb. It makes your world shrink to the size of a screen. it makes your calling feel unreachable, your faith feels faked, and your mission feel far away.

> And the most heartbreaking part? Some people will spend their entire teenage years, and even into adulthood chasing pleasure and missing their purpose. Not because they didn't love God, but because they were too chained to feel free.

5. Your Connection to God

This is the greatest loss of all.

Lust doesn't make God love you less. But it makes you feel less worthy of His love. You start skipping prayer. Worship feels distant. The Bible feels dry. You don't want to raise your hands at youth group because deep down you feel like a hypocrite. You want to feel close to God again, but something always feels "off".

That "off" is not God being far, it's sin standing in the way.

And the longer you stay stuck in secret sin, the harder it becomes to feel the presence of the One who can actually heal you. But here's the miracle of grace... Even when you've silenced your prayers, He hasn't silenced His pursuit of you. He's still calling. Still waiting. Still knocking

You haven't sinned too far.

You haven't failed too much.

You are not to broken to be restored.

But There's a Way Out!

You might feel trapped right now. You might feel like your soul is duct-taped to the sin you swore you'd quit. You might feel like you've been kneeling at the altar of lust for so long that you forgot what freedom tastes like. But I'm here today to tell you from my own experiences...

WITH GOD ALL THINGS ARE POSSIBLE

Not a shortcut. Not a magic prayer. Not a guilt trip. A real, raw, powerful rescue, offered by the living God who still breaks chains, and generational curses.

1. Call Lust What it is

Stop sugarcoating it. Don't call it "just temptation." Don't call it "just being curious." Don't call it "something all guys/girls deal with." Call it sin. Because when you name it for what it is, it loses its grip.

God isn't afraid of your honesty He already sees it all. Confession doesn't shock Him, it frees you.

"If we confess our sins, He is faithful and just and will forgive us our sins and purify us from all unrighteousness". 1 John 1:9

2. Bring it Into the Light

Lust thrives in darkness, it grows when it's hidden, whispered about, or ignored. But the moment you bring it into the light through confession, prayer, and accountability it starts to die. That's why the devil works overtime to convince you to stay silent:

"They'll judge you"

"You'll lose their respect"

"You can fix this on your own"

Lies. All of it.

True friendship doesn't pull away when you open up. They lean in. They pray harder. They walk with you. And if they don't? Then they're not the friends God sent.

"Confess your sins to each other and pray for each other so that you may be healed." James 5:16

You don't need hype. You need healing. And healing comes through honesty.

3. Cut Off the Source

Jesus didn't play games with sin. He said, *"if your eyes cause you to sin, gouge it out. If your hand causes sin, cut it off."* (Matthew 5:29-30)

Was He being literal? No. But was He being serious? Absolutely.

If your apps lead you to sin, delete them. If your phone leads you to sin, get a dumb phone. If a certain person, platform, or pattern opens the door, slam it shut!

Don't just say "I'll do better." Make war!

Freedom requires sacrifice. But that sacrifice is nothing compared to the joy of a clean heart and clean mind.

4. Get Real With God

When's the last time you cried out for purity?

Not just saying "sorry" but asking God to actually change you. To scrub your soul. To flood your mind with new desires. To make you hate what you once craved and crave what you once ignored.

He can do that. He wants to do that.

But He's waiting for you to get real. To drop the performance. To come to Him, not with excuses, but with a surrender. Because purity isn't about perfection, it's about proximity. The closer you walk with Jesus; the less power sin has.

5. Replace the Sin with Strength

Don't just remove the sin. Replace it.

- Replace screen time with Scripture time

- Replace late-night scrolling with worship music.

- Replace isolation with discipleship.

- Replace shame with Scripture memorization.

- Replace fantasy with real prayer and purpose.

Because your heart was made to hunger, and it will feed on something. If you don't fill it with truth, it'll run right back to lies.

"*How can a young person stay on the path of purity? By living according to your word*". Psalms 119:9

You can't just white-knuckle your way to holiness. **You have to replace the lie with the truth**, every single day.

This is Your Wake-Up Call

You don't need. to wait until you're older.

You don't need to wait till you "feel ready".

You don't need to wait till you've sinned one last time.

The time is now.

The grace is now.

The power of God is here, to restore, to redeem, and revive you.

> Lust doesn't have to own you. Your screen doesn't have to master you. You are not what you've done, you are who God is making you to be. And if he raised Jesus from the grave, then He can raise you out of this pit you may think is endless, but I know, and I want you to know it isn't with God on your side.

This is not your end. It's your beginning.

Reflection Questions

- When did lust first enter your life? Was it something you searched for or something that found you?

_____

_____

- How has your mind, your relationships, or your connection with God changed since then?

_____

_____

- What are places, apps, or habits in your life that trigger temptation the most?

_____

_____

- What lies a have you believed about yourself because of your struggle with lust?

_____

_____

- Who is one person you could talk to this week to bring your sin into the light?

_____

_____

Journal Prompt

Write a raw and honest letter to God. Tell Him everything, your struggle, your shame, your frustrations, your numbness, and your desire for freedom. Don't hold anything back. Let it pour out like a conversation, not a performance. Ask Him to give you new eyes. Ask Him to rewire your heart. Ask Him to make you pure again, from the inside out.

Memory verse

"*How can a young person stay on the path of purity? By living according to your word*". Psalm 119:9

Write this verse somewhere visible, on a mirror, in your phone notes, or on a sticky note by your bed. Let it be a daily reminder that God has already given the way, and it begins with His word.

Prayer

"Father, you still love me, I'm tired of hiding. I'm tired of running. I'm tired of pretending I'm fine when I know I'm not. you see everything I've done, and yet you still. love me. You still call me. You still want me. God, I want to be pure, not just in my actions but in my heart. I don't want to be addicted. I don't want to be numb. I want to feel you again.

So right now, I surrender. I lay this sin at your feet. Clean me. Heal me. Make me new. Give me the strength to walk in the light, the courage to confess, and the wisdom to cut off what's killing me. I choose truth over lies. I choose you(love) over lust.

In Jesus' name,

Amen"

Chapter 2: Addicted But Numb

Y ou didn't mean to get here. Nobody does. No one sets out saying "I want to get addicted." No one opens their phone for the first time thinking "I want to be numb to real love, real people, and real joy."

But then it happens, you start coming back to it, you start using it as a way to cope and to fill the void you should be filling with Jesus you're filling with lust, greed, and jealousy of wanting to be like those people you see on the screen.

Slowly. Quietly. Consistently.

You click once. You scroll twice. You repeat it three times, five times, twenty times. And before long, you're not just struggling, you're stuck. Worse than that, you stop feeling bad. Worse than guilt.... You start feeling **nothing** at all.

That's the trap of addiction. It doesn't just capture your hands. It hardens your heart.

At first, sin feels like a wildfire in your chest. Guilt then hits you like a freight train. Your heart races. Your stomach sinks. You say, "Never again". But then you do it again, and again, and again. And what once made you tremble, now barely makes you blink.

The truth is... Sin doesn't always kill you in one blow. It takes little chips off you in each little hit of dopamine, of the drug/alcohol, of the social media, the energy drinks (I suffer heavily on this one). It kills you silently, in things people wouldn't start noticing. But you do, you notice.

The Numbness isn't Freedom, its Bondage in Disguise

When you first start playing around with addiction, you start thinking "*hey this eases the depression, the pain, the urge*" then eventually you realize "this is making it worse" and some people sadly realize this too late. The side effects, the long-term effects, the deathly effects have set in. And they are not going anywhere. You also will have long term guilt. But I'm here to tell you by the grace of God: **God sets you free from the guilt!**

The devil attacks you slowly, he makes you feel nothing, and a person that can't feel something is easier to control. That's what addiction does. It hijacks your mind, senses. It trains your mind to crave darkness and your body to flinch at the light. You're not just addicted, you're desensitized. It's like standing in a burning house and not smelling the smoke anymore. That's numbness.

When Conviction Fades, So Does Clarity

When you first started walking with Jesus everything felt alive:

- Worship brought tears to your eyes.

- Bible verses jumped of the page.

- Church felt like a home.

- Sin made you sick.

But now?

- Worship feels like noise.

- The Bible feels dry.

This is the slippery slope of a numb, broken heart. You're still going through the motions, but the **meaning** is gone. You're not dead, but you're not fully alive either. You're in between. Lukewarm. Dull. Disconnected.

Jesus warned us about this:

"Because you are lukewarm, neither hot nor cold, I am about to spit you out of my mouth." Revelations 3:16

This isn't about Him being harsh. It's about Him calling you back to real life. Back to fire. To the passion of His love, and His joy He supplies us with. To purpose.

Numbness Makes You Settle

When your numb, you stop reaching for heaven and start settling for earth.

You stop praying boldly.

You stop dreaming spiritually.

You stop expecting God to move in your life.

You settle for sin because it's familiar.

You settle for fake pleasure because it's easier than the real healing (Drugs, Alcohol, Lust, Lying even).

You settle for shallow friends, fake smiles, and watered down faith. The kind of faith that will get you by, but you won't be able to live in the abundant life God has for you.

Deep down you know you were made for more that's maybe why you're reading this book. Because you're searching for something that fills that void that isn't dangerous to your souls, heart, mind, and body.

It's Not Too Late to Wake Up

If you feel numb right now... that doesn't mean God's done with you. In fact, it might mean He's just getting started. While writing this makes me feel a revival, and spiritual battle that we have already won because we have such a powerful God! We don't need to be lost, broken, or addicted because God comes for us as broken and heals us.

> The hollow feeling inside you? That emptiness? That subtle ache in your chest when you think about where you used to be with God? That's proof your soul still remembers what it's like to feel alive. And if your soul remembers, God can restore. He doesn't give up on numb hearts. He revives them.

All He's waiting for is a whisper:

"God, I don't feel you right now... but I want to."

That's not weakness. It's worship. That's not failure. That's faith. Because numbness isn't the end of your story. It's the beginning of your resurrection.

You were never made to feel nothing. You were made to feel the full weight of love, the depth of joy, the sting of conviction, and the fire of purpose.

The numbness you're experiencing. That's not how you were designed. That's what sin does. It silences your soul. It puts cotton in your spiritual ears. It hardens your heart until you can't even tell what's real anymore.

God has given me a task, a purpose; to tell you the truth:

You can feel again.

God doesn't just forgive you; He revives you. He breathes life back into the dead, dark places. He restores emotions that felt lost. He wakes up hearts that have been cold for years. If you've gone numb this is your resurrection call.

Addiction is a Lie Dressed in Comfort

Addiction doesn't show up looking like a monster. It doesn't knock on your door dressed in chains, yelling "Let me ruin your life!"

It comes as a whisper...

It shows up as a "quick fix".

A "harmless escape"

A moment of relief when the world feels too loud or too heavy.

It doesn't look dangerous.

It looks comforting.

But it's a trap

The Bait is Pleasure, The Hook is Pain

Addiction always starts with a promise:

- "This will help you relax"

- "This will make the loneliness go away."

- "Just one more time, then you'll stop"

- "You deserve this after the week you've had"

It plays itself off like a friend, like something that understands you when no one else does. But here's the truth: **sin never comforts you. It's just distracting you while it poisons you.**

It numbs the pain, but it never heals it. It gives you pleasure but then robs your peace. It says, "I'll make you feel alive," but then leaves you feeling emptier than before.

What kind of comfort leaves you:

- Ashamed?

- Anxious?

- Tired?

- Alone?

That's not comfort. That's bondage.

It Feels Like Control. But It's Slavery.

When you're addicted, you tell yourself you're still in charge.
You say things like:

- "I can stop whenever I want."

- "It's not that bad."

But deep down, you know: You're not in control. You're checking that site when you swore you wouldn't. You're picking up your phone without thinking. You're picking up that bottle, drinking your "problems" away. You're hitting your vape, looking for the "high". You're repeating the cycle even though you hate it. And every time you "go back," it gets harder to walk away. That's how the enemy works. he gives you just enough pleasure to keep you coming back, but never enough peace to actually satisfy you.

It's a loop. A leash. A lie.

Addiction Tells You You're Broken Beyond Repair

Eventually, the lie deepens. The devil doesn't just say, "come try this again." He says, "Look at this new site, this new trend, the new flavor, new "high"."

But **Jesus never speaks to you like that.**

He never labels you by your lowest moments. He doesn't define you by your past mistakes. He doesn't lock you in a prison of shame and say, "Get used to it."

Instead, He says: *"It is for freedom that Christ has set us free."*
Galatians 5:1

And that's the difference. The enemy says, "you're stuck." Jesus says, "get up". The enemy says, "you're too dirty." Jesus says, "I've already made you clean." The enemy says, "you're a slave." Jesus says "you're my son. My daughter. My beloved."

The Truth Beneath the Lie

Here's the truth:

You don't need what you're addicted to. It's not saving you. It's satisfying you. It's not helping you survive; it's slowly making you forget who you are.

And who are you?

- You **are not** your habits

    ○ You **are** a child of God

- You **are not** your cravings

    ○ You **are** fruitful in God's fruit

- You **are not** your history

    ○ You **are** set free by God's name

You are a **child of God,** created with purpose, bought by blood, and invited into freedom. So today, start looking at your addictions for what they really are:

Not a friend.

Not real comfort.

Not love.

It's a lie with makeup on. A cage dressed by pillows. But you were made to be free.

But here's a way out

You might feel stuck. Maybe you've tried to quit. Maybe you've cried on your bedroom floor, made empty promises to God, deleted apps, threw things away, swore up and down you'd never go back. But then, you went back. You picked that bottle up, hit the vape again, or even watched those videos again.

But here's the truth:

Addiction is strong-but Jesus is stronger.

There's a way out. And it's not through willpower. It's through surrender.

1. Admit You Can't Beat This Alone

This is where your revival will begin. Not with performance. Not with a perfect streak. But with some simple yet effective humility.

"God, I've tried. I can't do it on my own. I need you."

That's not weakness. That's what older people would say is wisdom ...

Because what you're battling is spiritual. You can't outsmart it. You can't outwork it as much as social media wants to tell you. You can only out-surrender it. Jesus didn't die so you could fight yourself into freedom, He died to break it Himself.

2. Drag It Into The Light

You might've seen a pattern in this chapter and the last. A lot of things in this book will be a pattern, because they all work. They all are proven methods to fight Lust, Addiction, Depression and all.

Sin feeds on secrecy. Shame grows in the dark. As long as you keep hiding it, it keeps winning. But something powerful, supernatural happens when you drag your addiction into the light. When you tell someone. When you speak it. When you say, "This is what I'm struggling with."

Scripture says:

"Whoever conceals their sins does not prosper, but the one who confesses and renounces them finds mercy". Proverbs 28:13 CSB

Notice it doesn't say they will be punished. It says they will find mercy. You're not meant to carry this alone. Tell a pastor. A godly friend. Yes, it's scary, it's something most don't have the strength to do and face possible repercussion. But if they are loving they are going to understand and want to comfort and help you. Healing begins with honesty. You don't need to be exposed; you need to be set free.

3. Starve the Flesh, Feed the Spirit

Freedom doesn't come by accident. It comes by decision. Daily. Even every second.

- Delete the apps.

- Cut off the access points.

- Set up filters or accountability software.

- Change the environment, not just place but friends that make you or entice you to do sinful actions.

- Replace temptation with the truth.

Don't just remove the addiction, replace it with something that takes the time, the guilt, and turns it into something you, everyone around you would be proud of.

- Download a Bible app

- Read scripture when cravings hit.

- Pray out loud when lies scream into your mind.

- Listen to worship music when you feel numb

- Memorize verses that anchor you when you're weak.

You're not just fighting a habit; you are rewiring the soul. And God is faithful to meet you in the middle of the process.

4. Don't Confuse Falling With Failing

You will stumble.

This is something I had to deal with, I would have a good couple weeks then I would be alone in my room and see something and instantly I would be back in the cycle of falling and hiding it. And it took a toll on my mental and physical health. The guilt you feel is real, it is not something to be belittled. It can affect you really bad. But remember that God is always there and *falling is not always Failing*.

Falling is a part of the fight. But God isn't keeping score, He's keeping His arms open. You may relapse. You may mess up. But here's what God won't do:

He won't give up on you

Every day you get up is a win. Every prayer you whisper is a strike against the enemy. Every time you choose obedience over shame; you're walking in freedom. Even if you limp your way forward, keep walking

5. Fix Your Eyes on Jesus, Not Your Sin

Here every time you fall back down, I want you to remember that Jesus died on the cross for you. He died for every sin, every fall, every time, every addiction, He knew what would happen if He didn't and that would be hell, but He died and that gave you eternal life.

If all you ever do is look at your sin, you'll stay stuck with it. But when you look at Jesus, everything starts to shift. You begin to realize:

- He's not mad at you.

- He's not disgusted by you.

- He's not shocked by your struggle.

- He's not rolling His eyes at your mess. Like some parents...

He's standing there in the middle of it saying:
- "Come to me"

- "Let me carry this"

- "Let me show you a better way."

He doesn't want you cleaned up; He wants you close.

And the closer you get to Him, the looser those chains will feel.

There is a way out. And His name is Jesus.

Not a religion. Not rules. Not performance. Just a person. A Savior. A Healer.

And He isn't that far away

He's right here. In your room. In your thoughts. In your weakness.

Ready to lead you out, step by step, breath by breath.

This chapter is not your prison.

It's your exit door.

Chapter 2 Closing: Wake Me Up Again

You've felt it, that heavy silence in your chest. The slow drift from who you were. That voice in your head that you first thought was yourself just going insane but it's really there, I may have it to, who knows, the voice says, "This is just how it is now". But you don't have to stay numb. You don't have to live addicted. You don't have to walk around spiritually dead inside. There is a way out. And there is especially a way back.

The God who met the prodigal in the pigpen... The God who breathed life into dry bones... The God who called Lazarus out of the grave...

Is the same God who's calling your name right now!

"Wake up, sleeper, rise from the dead, and Christ will shine on you."

Ephesians 5:14

Your numbness is not final.

Your addiction is not your identity.

Your story is not stuck.

You were made to feel again. To live again. To walk in freedom and passion and peace. And Jesus isn't waiting for you at the finish line. He's walking with you from the starting line.

TAKE HIS HAND. STEP FORWARD. LET HIM LEAD.

Reflection Questions

- When did you start feeling spiritually numb? What triggered the shift?

_____

_____

- What has addiction or repeated sin stolen from your life?

_____

_____

- In what areas are you still trying to fight alone?

_____

_____

- Who can you confess to or invite into your healing journey?

_____

_____

- What steps can you take this week to starve your flesh and feed your spirit?

_____

_____

Journal Prompt:

Write about the first time you noticed a change in your heart. Was it after a fall into sin? A moment of isolation? A time you felt like God didn't show up when you needed Him.

- What was happening in your life when the fire in your faith started flickering?

- What did your relationship with God used to feel like, and what does it feel like now?

- Are there habits or addictions that slowly crept in and stole your joy, peace, or sensitivity to God's voice?

End by writing this sentence-Honestly and boldly

"God, I want to feel again. I want you to wake up my soul, even if it hurts."

Scripture:

- Psalm 51:10

- Romans 6:14

- 2 Corinthians 3:17

- Isaiah 43:19

Prayer:

"God, I confess I've gone numb. I've let addiction, shame, and sin silence my spirit. But I don't want to stay this way. Wake me up again. Break the chains I've worn far too long. Restore what's been lost. Help me feel again, your love, your voice, your purpose. I can't do this alone. I surrender it all to you. Make me new. Amen"

Chapter 3: School is Not Safe Anymore

There was once a time when the school was a place of learning and shaping. A place of discipline, but also a place of fun and learning. Some schools even had the Bible as a primary book in their classrooms. It was where minds were sharpened, where curiosity was grown up, and where teachers could be trusted.

Now?

For many, school has become a battleground. A place with constant attacks from the enemy. A spiritual war zone where truth is silenced, morality is mocked, and the minds of the young are not trained, they're targeted. You walk into a building five days a week with lighting, dusty books, screens, blank stares. But behind all of it is something much deeper, much darker.

The defilement of innocence.

The Classroom Isn't Neutral Anymore

There was a time when school was considered one of the safest places for a child. Not just physically, but mentally, emotionally, and spiritually. It was a place where teachers could be trusted, boundaries were very clear, and parents had a voice. You might think you have voices as parents, but most schools really only do what they think is better for them.

Now?

The classroom has become one of the most dangerous places for a young person, especially a Christian.

Why?

Because it no longer aims to teach kids how to think, it tells them what to think, to be, and that they have choice on choices that shouldn't be made as a kid. And slowly, quietly, intentionally, it's been stealing innocence, planting confusion, and normalizing sin under the disguise of "education". The modern classroom doesn't stand in the middle anymore. It doesn't give both sides of the story. It's not neutral.

It has picked a side. And most of the time except a select few, it isn't Gods side.

Lies Are Being Taught Like Facts

Let's be real.

What's being pushed in today's curriculum isn't just information. It's an ideology, one carefully crafted to reshape the worldview and minds of the generation, my generation, your generation.

- Kids are taught that truth is relative, that they can define right and wrong for themselves.

- Gender is no longer rooted in biology or the gender you were born as, it is treated like a costume you change based on your mood, or the current trend.

- Lust is normalized while purity has become ridiculed.

- Families are redefined. Sin is celebrated. And God is either edited out or mocked entirely.

- Most families have a one parent household. Where in the Bible divorce or one parent houses were not normal, because it is essential to the child to have a father and a mother.

They don't just want you to learn about the world, they want you to see it through the lens that the snowflakes want to have people see. And if you speak up? You are called intolerant. Old fashioned. Brainwashed. Dangerous.

- All because you chose the Word of God over the wisdom of the world. The truth Jesus preaches compared to the falsehood the world preaches.

What You See Isn't All That's Happening

The danger in today's school isn't just in the books, or the literature, or the art. It's in the atmosphere. There's spiritual heaviness in some classrooms that you can't explain.

- You walk in and feel instantly anxious.

- You sit through lectures that make you feel small or invisible.

- You hear people say things that twist your stomach, not just because they're wrong, but because they're wrong.

That's not just discomfort. That's discernment. The Holy Spirit in you is warning you.

Because what's being normalized in schools today isn't just "freedom of expression", its often rebellion dressed up as progress.

Not just culture. It's warfare. And the enemy knows that if he can shape the classroom, he can shape the culture that comes next.

Teachers Are No Longer Just Teachers

There are still godly, kind, and wise teachers out there that are still trying to fight against the culture of today, no doubt. For example, in the first and second grades, Mrs Breaux and Mrs. Shipman were two major teachers in my life that guided thier class with godly principles that help shape me into the person I am today. They still have influence in my life as I regularly interact with them in many situations years after I was in their classrooms. But in many classrooms across the country the role of "teacher" has been twisted. We have teachers who are flying the pride flag instead of an American flag. American flags are coming down in schools all across our country.

Now they are not just teaching math or English.

- Some are pushing personal opinions about sex, race, politics, or gender onto kids who haven't even hit puberty

- Some are introducing graphic, inappropriate content under the banner of "inclusivity"

- Others are pressuring students to accept beliefs that directly contradict God's word, without ever calling it what it is.

Let's be clear: that's not teaching. That's targeting.

And when a teenager challenges it? Their called "disruptive", they're sent to the office, they're told that they are the problem. But all they're doing is standing for the truth.

Christian Teens Are Being Spiritually Isolated

Imagine being fifteen years old, walking into a classroom full of noise, pressure, and distraction. Trying to follow Jesus in a world that wants nothing to do with Him. You sit down quietly during pride month. You bow your head and pray before your lunch. You bring your Bible in your backpack. And somehow... you're the one that gets stared at like you're the threat.

You feel the stares. You hear the whispers. You feel alone

But here's the truth:

You're not crazy. You're not wrong. You're not alone

> You are a threat, to the darkness. Because light always exposes what's been hiding. The world doesn't hate you because of you. It hates you because of what you carry.

The System is Not for You, But God Still is!

You weren't meant to blend in with this system.

"Friendship with the world is enmity with God" James 4:4

That's not just a verse, it's a warning. The school system has been drifting away from God for years. And now it's sprinting. But you don't have to go with it. You were never called to go along with the current. You were called to walk on the water, and hey maybe you create some sort of splash along the way.

So even if your school feels like a battlefield, even if your teachers roll their eyes when you talk about Jesus, even if your friends mock your purity, your faith, or your conviction.

Stand your ground.

Because while the system may not be for you... Heaven still is and always will be. And God honors those who stand for truth when it would be easier to sit in silence

Surviving Spiritually In a Godless System

Let's be honest, being a young Christian in a modern school feels like walking through a storm without a shelter, without protection. You're not just fighting temptation. Your battling exhaustion. Pressure. Isolation. Confusion. And most days, it feels like no one gets it.

Your classmates are chasing attention. Your teachers avoid the truth. Your work ignores God. And somehow, you're supposed to keep your faith alive in the middle of it all. *Yes, yes you are.*

Because even when the system turns it back on God. He has never turned His back on you, or the system.

1. **Armor up Daily**

I will talk about this more in depth in Chapter 8 when I break down each piece of the armor of God. You're not just attending school. You're walking into a war zone.

That's why Ephesians 6 doesn't say "take it easy" it says:

"*Put on the full armor of God, so that you can take your stand against the devil's schemes*". Ephesians 6:11

You need protection. Not just from temptations, but from the lies you'll hear, the pressure you'll feel, and the atmosphere that wants to numb your spirit.

Before you walk into school:

- Pray over your day.

- Ask God to guard your eyes, your ears, and your heart.

- Read a short scripture, even one verse can hold your soul down.

- Speak truth out loud.

Because walking into school without prayer is like walking into battle without armor.

2. Choose Friends Like Your Faith Depends On it, Because It Does

You don't need a crowd. You need the right two or three. Even if it's just one person who loves Jesus, link arms. Sit with them. Pray with them. Talk real with them. Because isolation is the devil's playground, and silence breeds compromise. And if you don't have anyone yet. Ask God to bring them. He will. And while you wait, be that person for someone else. You might be someone else answered prayer

3. Speak Life, Even When No One Else Does

Your school is full of kids who are dying inside, but smiling in the hallways.

Some are addicted.

Some are suicidal.

Some are trapped in shame, abuse, and spiritual darkness.

They don't need more popularity or attention. They need **hope.**

And maybe... God put you in that classroom, that hallway, that school, to be the one who brings it.

Don't underestimate the power of a simple word:

- "Hey, I'm praying for you"

- "You're not alone"

- " Jesus still loves you, no matter what"

- "You can come sit with me"

That's not cheesy, or weird. That's warfare. Because you never know what chain can break by the words you speak.

4. Remember Who Sent You There

You're not in that school by accident. You might hate it. You might feel like you're just trying to survive it (I went through this, thinking "I'm just here to graduate"). But what if God placed you there? Not to blend in... But to bring light into the darkest places. Each day as you enter that building, you are entering one of the largest mission fields in the modern world. Embrace that you are there as missionary student sent by the Creator of the universe to make his Son, Jesus Christ known to those you encounter each day.

"You are the light of the world. A city on a hill cannot be hidden". Matthew 5:14

Even if it's hard. Even if you feel overlooked. Even if the system feels too far gone. You are not powerless. Because the same spirit that raised Jesus from the dead, lives in you. And one spirit filled student in a broken school is more powerful than an army of darkness.

Closing: Called to Be The Difference

School isn't just where you sit for seven hours a day, learning new things or like me just sitting there on your phone. It's where the enemy wages a war again your identity. Where the culture tries to rewrite the truth, where silence is safer than speaking up... and where most students feel like they're slowly drowning.

But you?

You don't have to drown.

You don't have to conform, compromise, or cave in. You don't have to let your voice go quiet or your spirit grow numb. You don't have to keep your head down and just try to get through. Because you were not made to survive the system, you were made to disrupt it and change it.

You were made to be the one who still believes in purity. The one who won't laugh at sin just to fit in. The one who stands when everyone else folds. The one who prays over their friends in secret, or even at lunch out loud. The one who walks into school like a missionary, not a victim.

You are not too young.

You are not too broken.

You are not outnumbered.

You have heavens backing. You have the Spirit inside you, and you have a purpose in the middle of the flawed system.

So don't just go to school.

Go in bold. Go in covered with prayer. Go in lit up with the truth.

*Me praying at my school's flagpole as a
seven year old boy*

And remember: When you carry the presence of God. Even the darkest hallways can't stay the same.

Mocked for Believing, Pressure to Conform

Being a Christian in today's school system can feel like walking through fire with no armor.

- You mention Jesus, and they roll their eyes.

- You say you're waiting for marriage, and they laugh.

- You bring your Bible, and they say your brainwashed.

- You say no to drugs or parties, and they say you're boring,

Your told to be "open-minded," but that only applies if you agree with their opinions, and the opinions vary each person. Your told to be "tolerant," but no one tolerates your faith.

The world has made it clear: **You can believe anything... as long as it's not biblical.**

A Generation Growing Up Too Fast

Back in my day...I'm the same age as the kids I am writing about; I am a sophomore in high school. About to be 16, and it feels like the 6th and 7th graders are turning out to be more grown up not in a good way then us high schoolers.

School used to prepare kids for adulthood. Now it is pushing them into adulthood to soon.

- Middle schoolers watching porn in the bathrooms.

- Sixth graders vaping in gym class.

- Teachers turning a blind eye while bullying destroys someone's will to live.

- Girls being pressured to send pictures. Boys being praised for being predators. Or the flip

And through it all the system stays silent.

It's not just dangerous... its demonic.

Because the confusion, the sexualization, the brokenness, is a deeper plan. To kill the purity of a generation that is supposed to cause an uproar against the devil. To harden their hearts before they even know how to pray.

Reflection Questions:

- What lies have I believed about school being "just a phase "or "not that serious"?

- How has my school affected my faith, positively or negatively?

- What's one area where I can take a bold stand for God this week?

- Who around me is hurting and needs encouragement or prayer?

- Have I been blending in or standing out? Why?

Prayer:

"God, you know how hard it is to be a Christian in school today. You see every moment I feel alone, mocked, or tempted to quit. But I don't want to blend in anymore, I want to be bold. Give me strength. Help me stand. Used me to bring light into this place. Fill me with your spirit every morning... Amen"

Scripture to Hold On To:

- Daniel 1:8, Psalm 119:9, 2 Timothy 1:7, John 17:15

Chapter 4: The Spirit of Depression

You wake up and feel nothing. Not anger. Not joy. Not pain. Just... empty. You stare at the ceiling and ask yourself why it's so hard to breath, why it's so hard to care? Your body is there but your spirit feels crushed. And the worst part?

You don't know how to explain it to anyone.

This is more than sadness. More than a bad day. This is war, and it is spiritual... the good news it has already been won by God.

We live in a world where depression has become normal. Where numbness is expected. Where hopelessness is joked about online but lived out in silence. Behind the statistics, behind the fake smiles, behind the videos, that joke about pain...

there's a spirit at work

And it's not from God.

When the Soul Goes Silent

There's a moment that no one talks about enough. It's not when the tears are falling, or the breakdown finally hits. It's the moment before that, when you stop caring. When your soul doesn't scream anymore. It just... goes quiet.

No passion.

No desire.

No hunger for the Word.

No energy to pray.

No tears left to cry.

You wake up, go through the motions, smile when needed, and shut down inside. That silence isn't peace. It's suffocation. Because depression doesn't always look like falling apart. Sometimes it looks like functioning while dying inside. Getting the grades. Showing up to practice. Making the jokes. But inside? You're gone.

The spirit of depression wants to drain you of hope, joy, purpose, and connection, until your faith feels fake, and your life feels pointless. And it's not random. It's targeted. Because when Satan sees that God is calling you to something greater, he doesn't just send temptation. He sends oppression. He doesn't want you to sin, he wants you to sink. Quietly. Privately. Until no one notices... until you can't even cry for help.

But God Notices

"The Lord is close to the brokenhearted and saves those who are crushed in spirit." Psalm 34:18

You may feel like no one sees you. Like the people around you wouldn't understand even if you tried to explain it.

But God does.

He sees the weight you carry that you never post about. He hears the thoughts that race through your mind late at night. He watches the way you force yourself out of bed and pretend you're fine. And He is not mad at you for being depressed. He's not disappointed. He's not ashamed of your struggle. In fact, Jesus Himself wept. Jesus got tired. Jesus felt sorrow so deep that it bled through His sweat.

> You are not broken beyond repair. You are just in a battle, and you were never meant to fight it alone.

The Darkness Has a Voice

Darkness doesn't just stay quiet. It speaks. It lies. And if you listen long enough, it starts to sound like your own thoughts:

"You're not enough"
"No one cares"
"This will never get better"
"You've already messed up too much."
"Just quit."
"Why even try?"

It's not just sadness. It's spiritual warfare, dressed in thoughts that sound familiar. That voice doesn't just aim to make you sad. It wants to pull you into despair, where hope feels foolish, and faith feels fake. It wants you to believe that your pain is permanent, and your prayers are pointless.

And sometimes, that voice disguises itself as logic:

- *"You're just being realistic"*

- *"You don't need to bother God with this."*

- *"Other people have it worse."*

- *"It's not even that serious"*

But it is serious. Because when you believe those lies long enough, they become chains. And here's what's even more dangerous:

The enemy doesn't just whisper lies. He uses your past wounds to reinforce them.

If you have been rejected, abused, overlooked, humiliated, forgotten...

He will use every scar to try to prove that he's right. That your life doesn't matter. That your prayers won't work. That God not listening. That the darkness will always win. But here's the truth, from the truth:

"He was a murderer from the beginning, not holding to the truth, for there is no truth in him. When he lies, he speaks his native language." John 8:44

Every word that voice speaks is a lie. Even the ones that sound the most convincing.

The Lie Behind the Smile

You know how to smile. You've trained your face to stretch just right. To make your friends think your fine. To keep your parents from worrying. To avoid the awkward questions from teachers, and youth leaders.

You laugh at the jokes. You show up to class. You post stories on socials. You even talk about God when it feels safe.

But inside?

You are drained. You are drowning. You are barely holding on.

This is what depression looks like for most people, its hidden in plain sight.

It's the athlete who won the game and had the greatest game of their life. But they cry in the locker room. It's the quiet girl who says she is just tired, but she's breaking down inside little by little by the criticism. It's the class clown who masks the pain with humor, who when they go home will sit with a razor blade asking themselves "why can't I ever make real friends or be myself around people." It's the worship leader who feels numb during the song they are singing.

The smile isn't fake, it's just survival.

Because the world tells us to keep performing, to keep looking okay, to keep pretending.

And in church? Sometimes the pressure's even worse.

We say thinks like:

- *"Just pray about it."*

- *"You have so much to be grateful for."*

- *"Don't let the enemy win"*

- *"You'll be fine. Just have faith."*

But the truth is, you can have faith but still feel pain. Pain doesn't discriminate. You can believe in God and still feel broken. You can love Jesus but still struggle to get out of bed.

My story of depression

I personally have gone through depression, when I was 11, my biological father, who had long line of anger issues, and a situation happened, and eventually he had pulled a gun on me and my grandma. I was the person who called the police on my own father. I, after the incident spent years of grief, blame, and anger, always blaming myself and telling myself I'm the reason he was like that. In 2024 I had to deal with getting broke up with by a girlfriend I had at the time, and it took a toll on me because she gave me the validation I should've been seeking from God and I went through weeks of self-harm, and suicidal ideations. I ended up on a bridge, and I stood up on the ledge and I heard I believe the voice of God speaking to me in my spirit saying "Don't jump, I still have plans for you." and that's why I am here today. I am constantly pursuing new avenues that God opens up because I know God has a plan for me and I want to live up to that plan.

Your smile might fool others, but it will never fool God:

"Man looks at the outward appearance, but the Lord looks at the heart."

1 Samuel 16:7

He sees what you don't say, He hears the prayers you only whisper in your mind. He knows the real story behind the smile, and He is not pushing you away. He is reaching for you. Because Jesus didn't come for the ones who had everything together, and who are not broken. He came for the ones who were sick, tired, lost, and hurting.

When the Pain Turn Inwards (Self Harm)

There's a moment when the pain inside becomes too much. And you start to wonder if hurting on the outside will make it feel lighter on the inside. It's not always about death. It's not even always about attention. Sometimes it is just about trying to feel something again or trying to make the pain stop screaming in your chest.

Maybe for you, it started small. Scratching, punching, biting, digging your nails into your arms. Then it started to grow, blades, burns, bruises you make sure no one sees. Not because you want to die... but because you don't know how to live with the aching inside your heart anymore.

Let's name it: **This is self-harm**

And it is not just a bad habit. It's not just a phase. It is not just a coping mechanism. It is a spiritual warfare that you are trying to fight alone.

"No one ever hates his own body, but he feeds and cares for it, just as Christ did the church." Ephesians 5:29

The enemy knows something. And that is if he can convince you to hate your own skin. To attack your own body, he doesn't even need to use someone else to hurt you. You'll do it for him. That is how dark and twisted this battle is.

Because your body is the temple of God (1 Corinthians 6:19). And the enemy wants to destroy that temple through pain, shame, and silence.

But Let's Be Clear: Hurting Yourself Will Never Heal Your Heart

You might feel a relief for a moment. You might even feel a strange sense of control. But the guilt will always come. The wounds don't fix the brokenness. And shame doesn't make the darkness go away, it makes it stronger. Self-harm is a trap dressed as a release. A lie dressed as relief. But you don't have to stay in it. I am here to tell you Jesus doesn't just want to forgive you; he wants to heal you. The scars, the thoughts, the cycle, the silence, He sees it all, and He still reaches for you

He's not disgusted.

He's not shocked.

He's not turning away.

"*He heals the brokenhearted and binds up their wounds*" Psalm 147:3

That includes physical wounds. That includes the one you gave yourself. That includes **you**.

The Lie of Suicide: A War Against Purpose

Suicide isn't just about wanting to die. It is about wanting everything that is painful to stop being painful again. The thoughts, the loneliness, the guilt, the constant voice in your head that says:

- "*You don't matter.*"

- "*You're to broken.*"

- "*Nothing will ever change.*"

- "*Nobody will miss you.*"

- "*You'll never be loved*"

Those are just dark thoughts. They are demonic attacks aimed at image of God inside of you. Here is the root issue with suicide:

It's not that people want to end their life. It is that they have lost sight of what life truly is, and their purpose.

And the culture we live in doesn't help.

We live in a generation, trained to chase performance, popularity, perfection, but never taught how to fight through the pain. So, when the pain hits hard, through heartbreak, trauma, addiction, abuse, failure, mental illness, we don't know where to take it.

We shut down.

We isolate.

And we start believing the lie: "Maybe the world will be better off without me."

Let's be clear though: That thought is not the truth. That thought is spiritual attack. One, sadly many teens have to go through, such as me. It is the enemy trying to destroy you before you realize your God-given purpose. He wants to take you out before you discover what God created you to become. Because if you ever fully realized how much power, beauty, and calling you carry, hell would tremble

Why Suicide isn't the Answer

The biggest lie suicide tells is that it will bring peace. But suicide doesn't end pain it **transfers** it. It puts your family in agony. It leaves your friends confused, broken, and haunted of "what ifs". It silences your voice in a world that desperately needed to hear it. And worse of all, it cuts off what God still wanted to heal. Your pain may feel endless, but it's not. Your storm may feel permanent, but it is not trust me!! With God the power of God, nothing is forever except His love and mercy for you!

"The Lord is close to the brokenhearted and saves those who are crushed in spirit." Psalm 34:18

God isn't afraid of your darkness. He is not distant from your struggle. He is not done with you.

Suicide takes what Jesus already died for, and says, "It's not enough" But it is enough, Jesus is enough. Not just to forgive you, but to restore you.

There is an Escape

You are not stuck. You are not beyond saving. You are not too far gone.

There is a way out, not through death, not through pretending, but through Jesus. your Lord and Savior.

Not religion. Not performance. Not just "positive thoughts".

A real savior, who steps into real darkness and pulls people out.

"*He brought me up out of a horrible pit, out of the miry clay, and set my feet upon a rock*". Psalm 40:2

That's who He is. That is what He does.

The pain you're carrying. He already felt it.

The lies you've believed. He already silenced them.

The shame that you wear. He already wore it on the cross...

You don't have to earn your way to healing. You don't have to clean yourself up first. You don't have to be strong enough, good enough, or brave enough.

You just have to say: "Jesus, I need you."

And He will come running!

So, What Does the Way Out Look like?

It's not always instant. Sometimes it's a process. But it's possible, and it starts with truth:

- Tell someone: Silence is the enemy's weapon. Break it. You don't have to carry this burden alone.

- Name the lies: Write them down. Say them out loud. Then speak the Word of God over each one.

- Feed your spirit: You can't starve your soul and expect to stay strong. Read scripture even when you don't feel like it. Worship when it hurts.

- Pray real prayers: God isn't looking for pretty words. He's looking for honest hearts. "God I'm not okay." And that is a holy prayer.

- Let people in: Isolation is a breeding ground for despair. Find a mentor, a pastor, a counselor, someone safe and rooted in Christ.

- Hold on: Just one more day. One more step. One more breath. Because healing is coming. And your story isn't finished.

> **You are not a Burden, You Are a Work In Progress.** You weren't made to carry this alone. You weren't made to die in the middle of your story. You weren't made to listen and fall into the darkness. You were made to walk in the light. To breathe deeply again. To smile again, not the fake kind, but the real one. The kind born from joy, not from survival.

And you will. By the power of Jesus, you will.

Because: *"He who began a good work in you will carry it on to completion."* Philippians 1:6

You are not hopeless. You're not done. You're held.

Closing: You're Still Here for a Reason

If you're reading this right now, you have made it! And that means something. It means the darkness didn't win. It means your worst day wasn't your last. It means, no matter what your past holds, God still sees a future worth fighting for.

Yes, the thoughts come.

Yes, the pain feels real.

But there's something stronger than all of it: **Truth**

The truth is your life is sacred.

The truth is your breath is borrowed from heaven.

The truth is, you are seen, chosen, and still being persuaded by a Savior who went to the cross to prove it.

The world may not understand what you've walked through. But Jesus does. And He's not finished with you. Let this be the moment you say: "I'm not giving up; I'm giving this to God."

Let this be the day you reach out. Let this be the page you remember when the next storm hits. Let this be the chapter that didn't end in tragedy-but in a turning point.

You're not reading this by accident. This isn't just ink on a page. This is a rescue. A revival. A beginning. And when the voice in your head says, "there's no way out," You'll look back and say: "There was. His name is Jesus."

Questions:

- What have I believed about myself during my darkest moments? Were those things true?

_____

_____

- Have I ever felt like I had to hide my pain behind a smile? Why?

_____

_____

- What are the lies the enemy has whispered to me, and what does God say instead?

_____

_____

- Have I ever harmed myself, or thought about ending my life? What led me to that point?

_____

_____

- What does it mean to me that God sees every scar and still calls me loved and chosen?

_____

_____

Journal Prompt:

"Write a letter to your past self on the hardest day you ever have had. Tell that version of you what you wish they knew.

Remind them they weren't alone. Point them to the hope you know now or the hope you want to believe in.grateful. And let Jesus

speak through your pen. Even if you're still in that dark place right now write the letter you need to read,Amen

Prayer:

Jesus, I'm tired, I'm hurting. Sometimes it feels like too much. But I know you see me. And for that I am grateful. I love you Lord, please help me, I need your help. I need you Lord.

In your name, Amen.

Chapter 5: Redefining Identity

The Assault on Identity

In this generation, confusion is celebrated, and clarity is attacked. Lines that were once clear, what it meant to be a man, a woman, a son, a daughter, a person with purpose are now blurred by culture, twisted by media, and dismantled in a classroom.

We are told;

- *"You are who you feel like you are."*

- *"Gender is fluid."*

- *""ruth is personal."*

- *"Purpose is whatever makes you happy."*

But here is the truth. None of this confusion is random

It is **warfare.**

"So, God created mankind in His own image, in the imagine of God He created them; male and female He created them." Genesis 1:27

From the beginning, God made us intentionally male and female, not as an accident, not as a social construct, but as a reflection of His own image. Satan's strategy has always been the same: attack the image of God.

If he can confuse your identity, he can cloud your purpose. If he can twist masculinity and femininity, he can destroy the beauty and order of God's design. If he can convince a generation that they were made without meaning, he can paralyze them before they ever live in their calling.

Masculinity isn't Toxic, Sin is

God didn't design manhood to be dominating, aggressive, or emotionally numb even. He designed men to lead with strength, to protect their children, wife, parents, friends with love, and to walk humbly with God.

True masculinity looks like Jesus:

- Gentle, but not weak.

- Bold, but not cruel.

- Humble, but not passive.

The world calls that toxic, God calls that holy.

Young men today are often told to sit down, be quiet, and stay out of the way. But God calls them to stand up, take heart, and carry His name with courage.

You were never meant to shrink back into comfort. You were meant to fight for truth, family, purity, and faith.

Femininity isn't Fragile, It's Fierce in Grace

God made women with incredible purpose, created to nurture, to lead with wisdom, and to reflect the compassion and beauty of the heart of God.

Biblical femininity isn't weakness. It isn't quietness for the sake of silence.

It is strength with softness.

It is warfare in worship.

It is the glory of God wrapped in dignity and strength.

"*She is clothed with strength and dignity; she can laugh at the days to come.*"   Proverbs 31:25

Women were never meant to become men. And men were never meant to become women. We were meant to be whole in who we are, walking side by side, each made in the image of God, equal in worth, distinct in design.

The Call to Live Set Apart

You are not just a product of biology. You are not just a set of preferences, feelings, or desires.

You are chosen.

"*You are a chosen people, a royal priesthood, a holy nation, God's special possession...*" 1 Peter 2:9

The world says, "Be whoever you want." God says "Be who I made you to be"

There is peace in that. There is purpose in that. There is power in that

Your Identity was Never Meant to Be confusing

The world shouts a thousand labels. But heaven speaks on identity: Child of God.

That is who you are. Not because you earned it. Not because you got it all right. But because Jesus gave everything to restore what sin tried to steal.

You are not lost.

You are not a mistake.

You are not something to be figure out.

You are **known. Called. Set apart.**

And it is time to walk in that

Culture Doesn't Define You, Christ Does

Everywhere you look, the world is handing out identity like it's something you can pick off the shelf.

"Pick your pronouns."

"Decide your truth."

"Follow your heart."

But here is the lie beneath that logic: If you can redefine yourself at any moment, then your identity is built on nothing. It is like writing your name in the sand and expecting it to stay after the waves hit. That is why so many people feel lost even after the "discover" who they think they are. Because true identity isn't something you can make up. It is something receive.

You don't find who you are by looking inside yourself. You find it by looking at the one who created you. And when you do, here's what you'll see:

- You were made on purpose.

- You were created in the image of God.

- You are not your temptation

- You are not your own creation.

- You are not your mental health battle.

- You are not your sin, your shame, or your sexuality.

- You are **redeemed, beloved,** and **called**, if you belong to Jesus.

The Attack on Purpose

If the enemy can't confuse who you are, he'll try to convince you that your useless.

"Your just another person."

"You don't matter."

"You'll never do anything meaningful."

But scripture is clear. You were made for such time as this. You were born into this generation for a reason. God didn't give you breath just to survive the system. He created you to **stand out, carry light**, and **bring heaven into dark** times. You are not background noise in history. You are God's instrument, chosen to live out something eternal.

"*For we are God's masterpiece. He has created us anew Christ Jesus, so we can do the good things He planned for us long ago.*" Ephesians 2:10

This isn't motivational packed into scripture. This is a spirituality reality. And when you believe that truth, the chains of this world fall off.

A War for the Soul of a Generation

This isn't just a cultural shift. It is a spiritual war, and it is after the hearts of teens, young adults, and even children.

- Boys don't know how to become biblical men.

- Girls are told womanhood is oppression.

- Everyone is told truth is hateful.

- And the gospel is being replaced with self-help booklets, and false freedom.

But the good news: we are not supposed to blend in as Christians.

We were made to be salt and light. We were made to be holy and whole. We were made to know who we are and whose we are. And anyone who ever felt confused, broken, ashamed, or unsure, you are not alone. I have felt that way. But you don't have to stay there.

Jesus is not afraid of your questions, He is not put off by the pain, He is not overwhelmed by the confusion. He is the anchor when identity feels unstable. He is the Shepherd when you feel lost. He is the one who says:

"*You are mine.*" Isaiah 43:1

Returning to Who God Says You Are

At some point, you have to come home. Not to religion, not to rules. But to the voice of your Father, my Father, the loving Father.

The world will keep shouting who it thinks you are:

"Too broken."

"Too confused."

"Too far gone."

" To weird."

"Not enough."

But God speaks something better. Something eternal. And it is time to return to His truth, because only the creator gets to name His creation. Here is the expanded verse the full version of Isaiah 43:1

"*Fear not, for I have redeemed you; I have called you by name, you are mine.* "Isaiah 43:1

You Are Who He Says You Are:

- You are made in the image of God- Genesis 1:27

    ○ You weren't made to reflect trends. You were made to reflect Him.

- You are a new creation in Christ- 2 Corinthians 5:17

    ○ Your past does not have final say. Sin doesn't get to define your future.

- You are chosen, holy, and dearly loved- Colossians 3:12

    - Not because you earned it. Because He said so.

- You are not your feelings- Jeremiah 17:9

    - Your heart may lie. God's Word never does.

- You are not alone- Deuteronomy 31:6

    - Even when no one else gets it, He stays.

- You are called- 1 Peter 2:9

    - Not to just exist. To declare, to shine, to stand.

This isn't just good news. This is freedom.

Let God Rewrite the Labels

Maybe you've worn some labels too long:

- "Failure"

- "Addicted"

- "Weird"

- "Ugly"

- "Broken"

Maybe someone else put them on you. Maybe you put them on yourself. But God is ready to tear those off and give you your true name.

Son. Daughter. Free. Forgiven. Whole. Warrior. Loved. Mine.

> When you know who you are, the world loses its grip. Temptation loses all pull. And shame loses its voice. Because when your identity is built on Christ, it can't be stolen, shaken, or redefined.

Truth and Love: What God Says About LGBTQ+ Identity

This generation has been fed the idea that sexual and gender identity are the deepest truths about a person. That your desires define you. That your feelings are sacred. That questioning your gender is brave. And that living out your truth is the only path to happiness. But what if that "truth" leads to more confusion, not peace? What if the freedom culture promises... is actually a chain?

God Is Not Silent on This

Let's be clear, God doesn't hate gay people. He doesn't despise those who feel like they were born in the wrong body. He doesn't shame those wrestling with same-sex attraction, confusion, or loneliness.

He loves them!

But He doesn't lie to them.

"*Do not conform to the pattern of this world but be transformed by the renewing of your mind.*" Romans 12:2

The world says:

"Love is love."

"Be whoever you want."

"If it feels right, it must be right."

But God says something better and that is:

Love is holy, not just emotional.

You are not a random identity, you are His.

Feelings can lie, but God never will.

Homosexuality in Scripture

God's word is consistent from Genesis to Revelation: sexual intimacy, relationships are created by God and designed for marriage between one man and one woman. Not a man and man, not a woman and woman, not a man who changed to woman and man, or a woman who changed to man and woman, or anything of the sorts. And especially not a man and woman and other people.

"Because of this, God gave them over to shameful lusts... men committed shameful acts with other men and received in themselves the due penalty for their error." Romans 1:26-27

"Do not practice homosexuality... it is a detestable sin." Leviticus 18:22

This isn't about hatred. or fear (homophobia). It is about holiness. God doesn't single out homosexuality, He lists many sins together: pride, greed, lust, idolatry, gossip, and more (1 Corinthians 6:9-11)

But what matter most is this:

"And that is what some of you were. But you were washed, you were sanctified, you were justified in the name of the Lord Jesus Christ and by the spirit of our God." 1 Corinthians 6:11

You can be set free.

You can be washed clean.

You can walk in truth, not shame.

Gender Confusion and God's Design

"Male and female He created them." Genesis 1:27

God did not make a mistake when He gave you your body. You weren't born in the wrong one. Confusion is real. Dysphoria is real. But truth is greater.

The world is saying:

Gender is a feeling.

You can switch between identities.

Be your own creator.

But that's the original lie from Eden:

"In fact, God knows that when you eat it your eyes will be opened and you will be like God." Genesis 3:5

We don't need to reinvent ourselves. We need to return the one who created us. Because peace comes not when we change our bodies, but when we surrender our hearts.

Grace for the Struggle

If this is your story... if you have struggled with these desires... if you have been in same sex relationships or questioned your gender. You are not disqualified from Gods love. You are not too far gone. You are not a mistake. But God will never affirm something that hurts your soul, no matter how normal the world makes it look. Jesus didn't die to make you comfortable in sin. He died to make you **new**.

The Cross is for Everyone

Straight people don't go to heaven. Gay people don't go to hell. Saved people go to heaven. And forgiven people are made whole. The ground is level at the foot of the cross. Everyone must repent. Everyone must surrender. And everyone is invited into the arms of a savior who says: "Come as you are. But don't stay there."

Closing: The Return to Who you Are

You were never meant to defined by your urges, your confusion, your pain, or your past. You were meant to be defined by the one who formed you, name you, and called you. This world will keep trying to rewrite your identity, until you no longer know where you end, and the noise begins. But there is one voice still calling out in the chaos.

The world offers empty freedom. Jesus offers real freedom. Freedom that doesn't just tell you what you want to hear, it tells you the truth and then walks with you through the fire of becoming who you were always meant to be.

You don't need to pretend anymore. You don't need to blend in. You don't need to chase labels that don't last. You are loved by the Father, redeemed by the Son, and remade by the spirit. And it is time to live like it. Because once you know who you are in Christ, truly know, no lie, no label, no trend, and no temptation can take that from You.

Reflection Questions

- What labels have you been carrying that didn't come from God?

  _____

  _____

- Have you ever struggled with your sexuality or gender identity?

  _____

  _____

- What does it mean to you that you are made in God's image?

  _____

  _____

- Do you believe God can love and change someone struggling with homosexuality? Why?

  _____

  _____

- What parts of your identity have been shaped more by pain than purpose?

_____

_____

Journal Prompt:

Where have I been looking for my identity outside God? What lies have I believed about who I am?

Prayer:

God remind me who I am in you when the world tries to tell me otherwise. Help me walk in your truth, not my feelings. Amen

Chapter 6:
Friends,
Followers &
False Teachers

"*F or the time will come when people will not put up with sound doctrine. Instead, to suit their own desires, they will gather around them a great number of teachers to say what their itching ears want to hear*".
2 Timothy 4:3

We live in the loudest generation in human history. Voices flood your ears every day, from friends in school, teachers in classrooms, and strangers on social media with millions of "followers." Everyone is saying something. Everyone is preaching a message. And most of it has one theme: "Do what makes you happy. You are the truth."

But here is the problem with that message: If you are the standard, then there is no standard. And when there is no truth above you, you end up lost inside you.

Influence is Discipleship in Disguise

You might think scrolling is harmless. That your "for you page" is just entertainment after entertainment videos. But every video... every quote... every clip that grabs your attention is shaping your worldview. Some people are being discipled more by influencers than by the Word of God. They don't know the Bible, but they know what the newest trend, newest sports news, newest cancellation. They don't spend time in prayer, but they will spend hours with people they never will meet, soaking in their values, ideas, and brokenness.

"*Walk with the wise and become wise, for a companion of fools suffers harm.*" Proverbs 13:20

TikTok Stars, YouTubers, even teachers, some with good intentions, some without are preaching the gospel of self.

It sounds good. It feels empowering. But it is a trap set by the devil. Because what sounds like freedom is often just a polished version of pride, rebellion, and spiritual blindness.

Not Every Voice Deserves Your Ears

The person you listen to are shaping the person you are becoming. We don't always realize it, but our minds are like should, and every voice, video, music, text is planting seeds. Some grow into faith. Others into fear. Some into truth. Most into deception. The danger is that false teaching doesn't always show up screaming "I'm a lie." It shows up sounding nice, affirming, spiritual. It says just enough truth to sound right but twists it just enough to pull you off course.

"They will turn their ears away from the truth and turn aside to myths." 2 Timothy 4:4

The Most Dangerous Lies Are the Ones That Sound Loving

Many false teachers, online, in media, and even in schools, don't use fire and brimstone. They use acceptance, tolerance, and emotional language. They preach a god made in our image. Not the God of scripture.

They say:

- God just wants you to be happy.

- If it feels good, it must be right.

- Love means never correcting someone.

- Truth is whatever you say it is.

But real love tells the truth, real truth confronts lies. And real teachers don't point you to themselves, they point you to Jesus.

So, ask yourself:

- Who am I letting speak into my life?

- Do their words line up with God's word?

- Do they lead me closer to holiness, or closer to compromise?

We live in a culture where everyone gets a microphone and not everyone with a microphone should be listened to. In fact, some of the most followed people online are the furthest from truth, yet their words are treated like the Gospel. They speak boldly, confidently, with passion and emotion. But emotion doesn't make something true. You have to understand this: The enemy doesn't have to always show up with horns. Sometimes he shows up with soft voice, a nice smile, a message that sounds loving but leads to chains.

"Satan disguises himself as an angel of light." 2 Corinthians 11:14

There are influencers and teachers, some of them in your schools, your workplace, and even in your church, who are not leading people to Jesus... they are leading people to self-worship, moral compromise, and spiritual confusion. And if you're not anchored in the Word of God, you will be swept away by their charisma, their "positivity", or their emotional appeal.

Discernment Is Not Judgement it is Protection

Sometimes Christians get scared to speak out or think critically because they don't want to "judge." But there is a difference between judgement and discernment.

- Judgement says, "I'm better than you".

- Discernment says, "I need to guard my soul."

God calls us to be discerning, to test every spirit, to compare every word to His Word, and to walk in wisdom.

"Dear friends, do not believe every spirit, but test the spirits to see whether they are from God." 1 John 4:1

The Fruit Reveals the Root

You can tell a lot about a voice by looking at its fruit.

Does the person you're listening to:

- Produce humility or pride?

- Lead you to repentance or rebellion?

- Encourage godliness or self-centeredness?

- Build you up in truth or flatter you in falsehood?

Some of the loudest voices in culture today are not calling you to holiness, they are calling you to comfort at the cost of conviction. They say, "You don't need to change. You are perfect the way you are." But the gospel says, "You are deeply loved, but you desperately need grace." God will always love you as you are, but He loves you too much to leave you that way.

Jesus Over Everyone Else

> At the end of the day, there is only one voice that never fails. One voice that speaks no lies. One voice that leads to real life.
> **Jesus**

Not every friend deserves to shape your beliefs. Not every teacher speaks truth just because they stand up and "teach" the class. Not every trend is harmless just because it is viral. If the voice you are following doesn't sound like Jesus, it doesn't deserve your ears.

"My sheep listen to my voice; I know them, and they follow me." John 10:27

Follow Me Culture vs Follow Jesus

We live in a world obsessed with being followed. It starts early now, middle schoolers chasing views, likes, and followers like their worth depends on it. Influencers rise to fame not because they speak the truth, but because they know you to command your attention. And the more attention they get, the more influence they have. That is why they call them influencers, they shape how people think, dress, act, speak, and even believe. But Jesus wasn't chasing that kind of influence.

He wasn't building a brand. He wasn't trying to go viral. He wasn't even trying to be liked by the world. He was calling people to lay down their lives.

"Then He said to them all: 'Whoever wants to be my disciple must deny themselves and take up their crosses daily and follow me." Luke 9:23

Just sit here for a minute and let that sink in. Jesus didn't say "follow me and I'll make your life easier." He said, "follow me and die to yourself." Die to your pride. Die to your sin. Die to your flesh. And in doing that, you will find real life.

The Culture Says, "Be Seen", Jesus Says "Be Faithful"

This generation I'm from, and the younger one is addicted to visibility. We want to be seen, heard, liked, reposted, and validated. But Jesus calls us to faithfulness in the quiet, even when no one is watching. He calls us to integrity, to obedience, to truth, even if it costs us our influence.

"*Woe to you when everyone speaks well of you, for that is how their ancestors treated the false prophets.*" Luke 6:26

If your goal is to be loved by the world, you will always be tempted to compromise. But if your goal is following Jesus, you will have to be okay with being misunderstood, unfollowed, and even hated. And that is not failure, that is faithfulness.

You can't Follow Jesus and Still Worship the Crowd

You have got to choose

- Will you follow the influencers who promise validation but preach self?

- Or will you follow Jesus who promises the cross but leads to eternal life?

The crowd will clap for your sin. Jesus will call you out of it. The crowd will cheer when you conform, Jesus will transform you to stand out. The crowd says, "You do you." Jesus says, "Come to me."

And at the end of your life, the crowd won't be there anymore. It will be just you and God. And what mattered most won't be how many people you had following you, or how many people liked you. But what will matter will be whether or not you followed HIM.

The Cult of Self vs The Call of Christ

The "follow me" culture doesn't just want your time. It wants your identity. Your feed is full of people saying, "this is who you should be," "This is how you should talk," "This is how you should live."

It rewards performance. It celebrates image. And it thrives on comparison. We start measuring our value based on likes, views, and follows. But none of those things reflect who you are in God's eyes. In fact, they often distract you from it. You were never meant to chase fame. You were meant to carry a cross.

Jesus didn't say "Build your platform."

He said:

"Lose your life for my sake and find it." Matthew 10:39

Don't get me wrong, if you build a platform and it is based on teaching the Gospel, and you are not asking for followers, likes, and you are trusting in God not relying on yourself, and not using it as a self-validating, that is. Okay.

You Become What You Follow

Every time you hit "follow" on someones social media, you open a window. You start to take in their beliefs, their priorities, their mindset, whether you realize it or not.

If you constantly follow:

- People who flaunt pride, you will grow in pride.

- People who normalize sin, you will become numb to sin.

- People who glorify self, you will begin to glorify yourself too.

But if you follow Jesus, really follow Him, you will become more like Him:

- More humble.

- More joyful

- More free.

Jesus isn't a brand. He isn't a trend.

He is a renewer. A rock. An identity. A **Savior**.

And following Him isn't trendy, but it is transformative.

You are Not Just A Follower, You're an Influencer Too

Even if you don't have thousands of followers, you are a constant influence on someone.

If you have little siblings, they are looking up and watching you. In my case, I have three younger cousins that look up to me and we are closely knit and I want to be a godly influence to them. Your friends notice your choices. People see how you carry yourself, how you respond to pressure, what you stand for.

> So, the question is: Are you pointing people to the real Jesus, or just fitting in with the world?

You don't have to go viral to matter in the Kingdom, you just have to be faithful.

Closing: A Voice Worth Following

We weren't made to chase clout. We were made to carry the cross.

Every voice you follow is leading you somewhere, either toward truth or away from it. You cannot follow every trend, every influencer, and every opinion and still expect to walk in the truth of Christ. Eventually you will have to make a choice. Not just once, but daily. A line In the song, *Voice of Truth* by Casting Crowns says, *"of all the voices calling out to me, I will choose to listen to the voice of truth."* Let that be your focus, listen to the voice of truth.

You will have to choose: Jesus over everyone else.

The voices you allow in your life shape your future. So, ask yourself often:

Does this voice sound like Jesus? Does it bring peace or confusion? Does it lead to life, or slowly drain it away?

There is a Shepherd whose voice still cuts through the noise. His name is Jesus. And He still says, "follow me."

The world offers applause.

Jesus offers eternal life.

Choose wisely.

Reflection Questions

- Who are the top five voices you listen to or watch regularly? Do their messages align with God's word?

_____

_____

- Have you ever believed something because it sounded good but later realized it was against Scripture? What was it?

_____

_____

- Are you more concerned with being liked or being faithful to Jesus?

_____

_____

- In what ways have you allowed social media to influence your beliefs, identity, or purpose?

_____

_____

- How can you begin to filter the voices in your life through the lens of God's truth?

_____

_____

Journal Prompt:

Take a few minutes and list the voices you've been following lately, friends, teachers, influencers or creators. Ask God to show you which ones are helping you grow and which ones are pulling you for away from Him. Write down what "following Jesus" means to you right now, and what it might look like In your daily choices.

Prayer:

"Jesus, help me recognize the voices that don't belong in my life. Teach me to hear yours above all else, and give me the courage to follow you even when it costs me the crowd. Amen"

Chapter 7: Rebuilding the Temple (You)

B efore we start the building, we must realize: You are the temple.

"Do you not know that your bodies are temples of the Holy Spirit, who is in you...? You are not your own; you were bought at a price. Therefore, honor God with your bodies." 1 Corinthians 6:19-20

God never designed you to live spiritually broken, emotionally, numb or bound by sin. He designed you to be whole, holy, and His. But what do you do when the temple has been down by compromise? What happens when addiction, lust, pain, or shame has burned down the foundation.

You rebuild.

Not alone, but by His spirit.

God Heals What You Bring to Him

You cannot rebuild something you are still pretending isn't broken. The first step isn't trying harder, it is coming to Jesus honestly. Not with filters. Not with fake strength. Just raw surrender. Jesus isn't afraid of your mess. He already paid the price for it. He is not standing back with arms crossed, He is kneeling beside the rubble, ready to restore you.

God does not heal what you hide. He heals what you hand over.

I personally have walked around spiritually limping, emotionally shut down, and filled with pain I thought I could never speak about. I put on a smile, posted the highlight reels, and went to church while secretly bleeding inside, all because I thought being real would make me unworthy of God. But here is the truth: God is not repelled by your wounds; He is drawn to them. It has taken time for me to realize this.

Jesus did not die for the cleaned-up version of you. He died for the real. The version that is hurting. The version that fell again. The version that feels like they will never get it right. And here is the crazy grace of the gospel: **He still wants you**. Not after you fix yourself. Not after you prove something. Right now.

"Come to me, all you who are weary and burdened, and I will give you rest." Matthew 11:28

That is an open invitation to the broken, the addicted, the ashamed, and the tired. But you have to come! You have to bring Him what you are carrying, your guilt, your shame, your sin, your secrets, your trauma, and your numbness.

When you do, He doesn't shame you. He **covers** you. He does not expose you to mock you. He exposes to heal.

Think Jesus and the Leper

In Mark 1, a man with leprosy, a disease that made people outcasts that represented being unclean, comes to Jesus, falling to His knees. He doesn't hide. He doesn't pretend. He just says: "If you are willing, you can make me clean." His leprosy in that day was thought to associated with some sin which coming in contact with a leper made you unclean.

And what does Jesus do?

"Jesus reached out his hand and touched the man. 'I am willing,' he said, 'be clean!' Immediately the leprosy left him" Mark 1:41-42

Let this sink in: Jesus touched what others avoided. He wasn't afraid of the man's disease, and He is not afraid of yours. But notice what had to happen first: The man came to Jesus. He brought his pain. His uncleanness. His desperation. That is what rebuilding looks like. It doesn't start with strength. It starts with surrender.

God Doesn't Heal Masks. He Heals People

You don't have to fake it with God. He already knows everything and still invites you into healing.

- Bring Him your confusion.

- Bring Him your failure.

- Bring Him the heartbreak you never told anyone about.

- Bring Him the habit you feel chained to.

- Bring Him the lie you believed about yourself for years.

Healing begins when hiding ends.

The enemy wants you to believe that if people knew the real you, they would reject you. But God already knows the real you, and He calls you beloved. If you are willing to bring it to Him, God won't just patch up your life, He will make you new. That is His promise

"If anyone is in Christ, he is a new creation; the old has gone, the new is here!" 2 Corinthians 5:17

Purity: Not Perfection, but Surrender

When people hear the word "Purity", they usually think of sexual, lists of do or don'ts, or something only good kids care about. But real purity isn't about being spotless from never messing up. It Is about being surrendered to God daily, even when you have messed up. Purity is not just about your body. It is about your mind, your heart, your motives, your media, your relationships, your dreams. It is about living in a way that says "God, you can have all of me, because I trust that your way is better."

This is one way you can build up your temple. You are a living breathing temple created from God, by God, for God.

Purity leads to clarity. When your heart is pure, you start to see God more clearly. It isn't about being good enough. It is about being willing to be set apart, even when no one else is.

Prayer: Where Real Construction Happens

You cannot rebuild without staying connected to the architect.

Prayer is more than a spiritual task; it is spiritual oxygen. We often think prayer is only for the "super spiritual", the pastors, the people who don't struggle like we do. But that is a lie. Prayer was made for the desperate. The confused. The hurting, People just like you. Prayer is not about being perfect. It is about being present with God.

The Enemy Wants You Silent

Let's be honest, when you are ashamed the last thing you want to do is talk to God. That is by design, the enemy knows if he can get you to stay silent, he can keep you stuck. But prayer is the one thing Satan cannot hijack. It is the place where guilt dies, where shame is crushed, where chains break in the invisible. You may not "feel" God at first. You may not have the right words. But even a groan, even a whisper, even tears on your pillow, those are prayers that He hears.

"In the same way the Spirit helps us in our weakness... the Spirit himself intercedes for us through wordless groans." Romans 8:26

Prayer is not a ritual, it is a relationship

Imagine trying to rebuild a house without ever speaking to the builder. No communication would make it impossible to complete the house if the builder did not know what you wanted and what you expected. That is what life Is like without prayer. Prayer is your connection point to the God who knows every blueprint for your future.

It is where:

- You hear His direction.

- You feel His peace.

- You trade anxiety for clarity.

- You stop fighting alone.

You don't need fancy words. You don't need a church. You don't need the right background music. You just need to show up, heart open.

Closing: The Foundation Is Christ

You were not meant to live broken. You were not meant to fake it. You were created to be a temple of God's spirit, strong, holy, and full of purpose. The world may have handed you sin. Pain. Shame. But Jesus offers you healing, cleansing, and restoration. He doesn't ask you to rebuild your life alone. He simply says, "Come to me." Start there. And every day after that, keep coming back. Keep surrendering. Keep laying brick by brick in prayer, purity, and community and repentance. This is not about being perfect. It is about staying in His presence long enough to be made new. You are not a lost cause. You are a temple under construction, and the builder is faithful.

Reflection Questions

- What area of your life do you still try to hide from God instead of handing it over?

_____

_____

- How has your view of purity been shaped by culture, and what is God showing you about true purity?

_____

_____

- What is keeping you from praying more honestly and consistently?

_____

_____

Journal:

"God, I give you the broken parts of my life, the things I have tried to fix or hide on my own. Write down the things.

Prayer:

"Father, I surrender my brokenness to you, every part I have tried to fix without you. Rebuild me with your truth, your purity, and your presence and make me whole again in you"

Chapter 8: Spiritual Warfare 101

R eal battle. Real weapons. Real victory.

There is a reason your soul feels under attack. There is a reason why lust keeps knocking. There is a reason why depression won't leave. There is a reason why your attention drifts when you try to pray or open your Bible. It is not just mental; it is not just emotional.

It is spiritual.

And it is not a metaphor. It is a war. You were born into it. Every day you wake up, whether you realize it or not you step into a battlefield. But here is the truth: You are not powerless. You have been given armor, weapons, and authority in Jesus' name.

The Fight is Real

"*For our struggle is not against flesh and blood, but against the rulers, against the authorities, against the powers of this dark world and against the spiritual forces of evil in the heavenly realms.* Ephesians 6:12

Your battle isn't with your parents as much as you think it is. It is not with your anxiety. It is not with school, or friends, or even yourself. You are up against a real enemy who wants to steal your peace, choke your purpose, and drag your soul away from God one distraction a time. But the enemy is a defeated liar. Jesus already won the war at the cross. Now you have been called to stand in that victory, but you cannot do it half asleep or half surrendered.

Armor Up: Ephesians 6:10-18

I know we went over this verse shortly earlier in the book, but this goes into depth.

1. **Belt of Truth**

- Culture is full of lies. This belt holds everything together. God's truth keeps your identity, sexuality, value, and direction from falling apart.

2. Breastplate of Righteousness
- You are not protected by how good you are, you are protected by Jesus' righteousness covering your heart. When shame comes knocking, the breastplate reminds you: I've been made right by Christ.

3. Shoes of the Gospel of Peace
- Peace isn't passive. It is power. You walk into dark places not with fear, but with the peace of Jesus, ready to bring some good news wherever your feet go.

4. Shield of Faith

- When doubt flies like arrows, when thoughts whisper, "God left you," "You'll never be free.", faith lifts up and says: "I trust my God even when I can't see."

5. Helmet of Salvation

- The enemy favorite target is your mind. This helmet protects your thoughts. You're saved. You're loved. You belong to Jesus.

6. Sword of the Spirit

- This is your only offensive weapon. You don't just defend against lies; you strike back with scripture. When Jesus was tempted in the wilderness, He didn't argue, He quoted truth.

Even at an early age I was taught to armor up

Real Weapons, Not Trends

This fight won't be won by vibes, crystals, manifesting, or social media debates. You fight spiritually with spiritual weapons.

- **Fasting**: Weakens the flesh and strengthens your spirit.

- **Prayer**: Moves heaven and silences hell.

- **The Word:** Cuts through lies with divine truth.

- **Discernment**: Helps you spot the subtle schemes of the enemy.

This isn't about being extra religious. It is about being fully aware of your position in Christ, and your power to stand firm.

"*The weapons we fight with are not the weapons of the world... They have divine power to demolish strongholds.*" 2 Corinthians 10:4

I have had to battle literal demonic spirits in my life. It's crazy sounding, but I have encountered an evil spirit that has harassed me and done it's best to defeat me. I belong to God! Satan or his demons cannot possess me. The Bible tells us that we do battle these types of spiritual forces in our lives that seek to cause us to slide into old ways. Pray for me as I battle these forces in my life

Let's get into those 4 weapons above.

1. Fasting- Weakening the Flesh, Strengthening the Spirit

Fasting isn't a trend. It is spiritual discipline Jesus assumed His followers would practice.

"*When you fast...*" Matthew 6:16

Not if but when.

Fasting is more than skipping meals. It is saying "I need spiritual food more than physical food." It silences the flesh and tunes your spirit to hear God more clearly.

When you fast:

- Temptation weakens

- Your focus sharpens

- Heaven draws near

Fasting breaks addictions. Fasting renews your mind. Fasting says, "My appetite doesn't run my life, God does."

2. Prayer- More than talking, it is war

Prayer isn't a soft, cute habit. It is warfare. When you pray, you are not just venting. You are inviting heaven into the battlefield.

"*The prayer of righteous person is powerful and effective.*" James 5:16

Hell trembles when you pray. Chains break when you pray. Your identity gets rebuilt, your soul gets restored, and your enemies get silenced when you stay in constant communion with the Father. Prayer should be your first weapon, not your last resort.

3. The Word- A Weapon, not just a Devotional

You don't just read the Bible to "get inspired." You read it to arm yourself with truth that cuts through every lie

"*Take the sword of the spirit, which is the word of God.*" Ephesians 6:17

When Jesus was tempted in the wilderness, He didn't have a worship playlist or a podcast. He had scripture memorized and ready.

> If you don't know the Word, you will fall for anything that sounds good. The enemy twists the truth. He won't come at you with a red pitchfork, he will come wrapped in half-truths, desires, distractions, and friendly faces.

Know the word. Speak it. Declare it. Fight with it.

4. Discernment- The Eyes of the Spirit

Discernment isn't paranoia, it is protection.

It is that check in your spirit that says, "This looks right, but something's off." It is the wisdom to say no when everyone else says yes. It is the maturity to know that not every "spiritual" thing is godly.

"*Test every spirit... hold on to what is good, reject every kind of evil.*" 1 Thessalonians 5:21-22

You need discernment to recognize:

- False teachings dressed as "positivity"

- Manipulation hidden in relationships

- Hidden sin behind a good image

- And even the difference between your emotions and God's voice

Discernment keeps you from stepping into traps wrapped in "truth."

Trends Die. The Word Endures.

The weapons of God don't expire. They don't depend on likes, aesthetics, or cultural relevance.

- Fasting cuts through fog.

- Prayer invites divine power into human weakness.

- The Word crushes the lies of the enemy.

- Discernment keeps you from building your life on sand

So, stop fighting a spiritual war with cultural bandages. Your soul is too valuable. Your calling is too costly. Your God is too powerful.

The Authority of Jesus' Name

There is no name like the name of Jesus.

Not Buddha. Not Allah. Not crystals, not the universe, not a vibe, not energy. Not "your truth." Only Jesus Christ holds the power to make demons flee, break chains, and bring the dead to life, spiritually and physically.

"Therefore, God exalted Him to the highest place and gave Him the name that is above every name, that at the name of Jesus every knee should bow." Philippians 2:9-10

This is not religious hype. This is raw authority. When you speak the name of Jesus in faith:

- Fear must back down.

- Demons must leave.

- Lies lose their grip.

- Hope floods in.

- Heaven leans in.

It is Not a Magic Word, It is a Legal Power

Jesus' name isn't a spiritual password. It is not something you slap on the end of a prayer like punctuation. His name carries weight because of what He did:

- He lived sinless.

- He died in your place.

- He rose from the grave.

- He defeated sin, death, and hell forever.

And when you belong to Him, you carry His authority.

"I have given you authority to trample on snakes and scorpions and to overcome all the power of the enemy...". Luke 10:19

Jesus didn't die just to get you into Heaven. He gave you His name so you could walk in power on earth, right now. You don't have to be a pastor or a Bible scholar to use that authority. If you are a child of God, you have the right to use the name of Jesus in battle.

What Happens When You Use His Name

- When you say, "In Jesus' name, I rebuke the spirit of lust," that isn't you being dramatic. That is you stepping into kingdom authority.

- When you pray over someone and say, "Be healed in Jesus' name," You are speaking on behalf of the Great Physician.

- When you feel darkness creeping in and whisper "Jesus" You are lighting a fire the enemy cannot put out.

Hell trembles when His name is spoken in faith and submission

"*And these signs will accompany those who believe: In my name they will drive out demons...*". Mark 16:17

Why the World Hates His Name

Ever notice how no one gets offended if you say "God," "higher power," or "the universe"? But say "Jesus" and everything shifts?

Because the enemy isn't afraid of vague spiritually. He is terrified of the name hat conquered him. That is why the world tries to silence that name. That is why culture mocks it, censors it, replaces it. But you? You don't have to be silent. You speak that name boldly.

I love listening to all kinds of music and love Christ centered worship music. A favorite of mine when I was going through my mental spiral was the song by Katy Nichole, *In Jesus Name.* I still find comfort and am reminded of the power of God when I listen to her song.

Call on His Name. Carry His Name. Trust His Name.

Jesus' name is:

- Protection in the storm.

- Power in the fight.

- Peace in the chaos.

- Freedom from sin.

- Hope when you feel done.

So, speak it out loud. Whisper it in your weakness. Declare it in your room. Write it on your hear. Cling to it in temptation. And carry it like a sword.

Because the battle you're fighting? His name already won it.

Closing: Stay Ready

You weren't made to live weak, confused, and constantly defeated. You were made to stand, to fight, and to win, not in your own strength, but in the power of Jesus Christ. This war isn't coming someday, it is here now. But you haven't been left unarmed. You've been given everything you need to fight: Truth. Righteousness. Peace. Faith. Salvation. Scripture. Prayer. Fasting. And the name above every name.

The enemy wants you passive, distracted, and spiritually asleep. But God is calling you to wake up. To armor up. To step into the fight with boldness and confidence.

You don't have to be perfect. You don't have to know everything. You just have to say yes to the fight and trust the one who already won.

"Finally, be strong in the Lord and in His mighty power." Ephesians 6:10

Now, stand. Speak. Fight. Because you were born for this.

Reflection Questions

- What spiritual "trends" or habits have you leaned on in place of God's real weapons?

_____

_____

- Which piece of God's armor (Ephesians 6:10-18) do you feel you've neglected the most?

_____

_____

- Who are you fighting for beside yourself? Who in your life needs you to fight spiritually for them?

_____

_____

Journal Prompt:

Write about a time when you felt spiritually weak or attacked. How did you respond in that moment, and what could you have done differently using God's weapons? Ask God to reveal the real battle around you and awaken you to your authority in Christ.

Prayer

"Jesus, I don't want to fight with fake weapons anymore, I need your power and presence. Teach me to wear your armor, wield your name, and walk in victory every day."

Chapter 9: Revival Starts with You

D on't wait until later to carry the fire.

"Don't let anyone look down on you because you are young, but set an example for the believers in speech, in conduct, in love, in faith and in purity" 1 Timothy 4:12

You are Not Too Young, You are Right on Time

Some people wait for a stage, some wait for a degree, some wait till they "figure it all out." But revival doesn't start with a title. It starts with a heart that says: "God, use me, right here, right now." You don't need a mic to preach. You don't need a platform to lead. You don't need age to qualify what only **God can ignite**. All He needs is a willing flame.

The world says: "Wait for your turn."

God says: *"I made you for this moment."*

You don't need to be older to be dangerous to the kingdom of darkness. You don't need a résumé to be used by God. You just need a heart that says yes. David didn't wait until he was king to fight. He showed up to the battlefield with a sling, a few stones, and faith bigger than a giant. Everyone saw him as a little boy, but God, God saw him as a warrior.

Jeremiah tried to disqualify himself because of his age too:

"Alas, Sovereign Lord, I said, 'I do not know how to speak; I am too young.' But the Lord said to me, 'Do not say, 'I am too young.' You must go to everyone I send you to and say whatever I command you." Jeremiah 1:6-7

God didn't make you young so you'd be weak. He made you young so you would be bold, unshaped by fear, unashamed of truth, unafraid to run after what matters. While everyone else is scrolling, chasing influence, or numbing out, you have the chance to wake up and step into something eternal.

God Has Always Used the Young

- Joseph was 17 when God gave him a dream.

- Esther was a teenager when she risked everything to save her people.

- Josiah became king at 8 and led a revival by age 16.

- Mary was likely 14 or 15 when she was pregnant with Jesus.

- The disciples Jesus called. Some of them may have been teenagers

You see, God isn't waiting for you to outgrow your youth. He is calling you to steward in it. Because your youth is still raw and real. Your heart hasn't been dulled by decades of doubt. You are still moldable. Teachable. Dangerous. Remember, you are only young for a season of your life. God is preparing you for how He will use you for many years to come.

You are the Perfect Age for This Generation to Need You

You might think you are too young to make a difference. But the truth is, you are the exact age this broken, distracted, confused generation needs.

Why?

Because they will listen to you before they listen to a pastor in a suit. Because you speak the same language they do. You sit next to them in class. You walk the same halls. You scroll the same apps. You hear the same lies. And that means when you stand out, it is impossible to ignore. You are relatable and redeemed. Close in age but set apart in age. That is exactly why God is calling you now

Your Generation isn't Hopeless, It is Hungry

The world loves to talk down about Gen Z and Alpha:

- "They are all addicted to their phones."

- "They have no attention span."

- " They don't want God."

- "They are too far gone."

But look again.

Your generation isn't rebellious at the core, it is starving for something real. Real love. Real truth. Real purpose. Real power. And if you've experienced that in Jesus, you have what they are looking for. They don't need another filter, they need the fire of God. And maybe, just maybe, you are the one God is calling to carry it.

Revival Is Loudest When It Is Lived, Not Just Preached

> People your age are not looking for more religion. They are watching to see if anyone their age is actually living this thing out. You don't have to be loud to be effective. You just have to be real.

- Real in your walk.

- Real in your repentance.

- Real in your love.

- Real in your courage to say, "Jesus is the only way."

That kind of fire? It spreads. Fast.

You may never stand on a stage, but when you walk into a classroom, or a locker room, or even your friend group carrying the prescience of God, that is revival.

The Awakening of the Lost

Revival is not just about a room full of people worshipping. It is about the lost being found, the addicted being set free, the numb feeling again, and the ashamed finding grace. There are people all around you who are spiritually bleeding out, and they don't even know it. They laugh in the halls. They post perfect stories. They joke about being "dead inside" like it is funny. But behind the smile?

- Trauma.

- Loneliness.

- Secret Sin.

- Identity confusion.

- Anxiety they can't name.

- Thoughts of ending it all.

And here you are. Not by accident, not just observing, but called.
You carry life.
You carry light.
You carry the only message that saves.
"For the Son of Man came to seek and to save the lost." Luke 19:10
Jesus didn't come for the polished. He came for the broken, and He sends you to go after them.

It is Not About Being Loud, It is About Being Available

You don't need all the answers to reach the lost. You just need to show up and care enough to say something.

- Invite them to church.

- Sit with them when they're alone.

- Text them when God puts them on your heart.

- Share your story, no matter how messy it is.

- Pray out loud for them, even if your voice shakes.

You are not their Savior, but you know who is. And revival begin the moment you stop waiting for someone else to go, and you say.
"Here I am. Send me." Isaiah 6:8

They are Not Too Far Gone, And Neither Are You

The same God who pulled you out of darkness wants to do the same for them. And if you feel unqualified? Good. That means you will rely on Him. Because revival doesn't start with perfection. It starts with compassion. The revival of the lost begins when someone decides: "I can't let them die not knowing there is a better way." That someone might be you.

You Carry the Spark, Let it Burn

You don't need to see fire fall from Heaven to start a revival. Sometimes revival begins with a whisper:

"God, use me"

That whisper is a spark. And when surrendered, that spark becomes a wildfire, not just in your life, but in the lives of everyone around you. But here is the truth most people won't tell you: Sparks die when they are hidden. If you keep what God is doing in you locked away, too afraid, too ashamed, to comfortable, it'll fade.

You were never meant to just carry the spark. You were meant to make a flame from it.

"For this reason, I remind you to fan into flame the gift of God..." 2 Timothy 1:6

It Will Cost you Something

Revival will cost you comfort. It might cost you popularity. It will probably cost you your pride. My papaw has always told me that nothing in life is free.   Guess what? Being of fire for Jesus is going to cost you, be prepared. But what will you get in return?

- The presence of God

- A boldness you've never known

- Souls saved through your obedience

- Freedom in your own life

- A deeper, unshakeable faith

This generation doesn't need more cool Christians. It needs people are on fire. People who have seen the real Jesus and can't stay quiet about Him.

What if it starts with you?

You have been waiting for someone else to go first. But maybe God is asking you to be the first. To light the match. To make the call. To walk up to the friend who has been spiraling. To start the prayer group. To stop flirting with compromise and go all in. You don't have to know how it will all play out. You just need to burn. Because when one young person burns for Jesus, it ignites something in others. And before you know it, what started as a spark becomes a movement.

Closing: Don't Wait, Burn Now

Revival doesn't come when the conditions are perfect. It comes when hearts say yes. The same God who called Jeremiah, raised up, and filled the upper room with fire is still moving, and He is not waiting for tomorrow's leaders. He is calling you today. You don't have to have it all together. You just have to be surrendered. You just have to burn. This world doesn't need more opinions. It needs young men and women of conviction. It needs a generation that says:

"Jesus, you can have my schedule, my dreams, my voice, my purity, my reputation, use it all for your glory."

Don't wait until you're older. You are not too late. You are exactly who God wants, right now.

So, rise, shine, and BURN!

Reflection Questions

- What lie have you believed about your age, or ability to be used by God?

_____

_____

- Who in your life is spiritually lost and needs the light of Christ through you?

  _____

  _____

- What is one bold step of obedience to feel God is calling you to take this week?

  _____

  _____

- Are you hiding your fire out of fear or insecurity? Why?

  _____

  _____

- What would it look like for revival to start with you, in your room, school, or friend group?

  _____

  _____

Journal Prompt:

"God, I don't want to wait for someone else to lead, I want revival to start with me. Use my voice, my life, and obedience to light a fire in this generation. Even if it costs me something, I choose to burn for you."

Prayer:

Jesus, I give you all of me, my age, my voice, and my future. Let revival start in my heart and spread through my life, one act of obedience at a time.

Chapter 10: A Letter To the Next Generation

A s you are read this, please know, it is your turn.

Dear brother.

Dear sister.

Dear son, daughter future warrior of the kingdom.

I don't know your name yet.

I don't know your story.

But I do know this:

God's hand is on you.

You were born for more than survival. More than scrolling. More than performance and pressure and pretending you are okay. You were born for war, for worship, and for revival.

I Know it is Hard

The world you are stepping into is heavy. Louder. Faster. Darker than ever.

Sin in normal. Truth is twisted. Everything that is holy is mocked. And you are being told to stay quiet, just blend in. But here is what I need you to hear:

Don't you dare shrink back.

You don't need to look like them.

You don't need their approval.

You don't need to chase what they are chasing.

You were made to stand out, because you carry something eternal.

Take the Fire and Run

This letter isn't just encouragement. It is a torch.

Someone lit it before you. Someone burned for God in their time. Now they are handing it to you.

Don't let the fire die in your hands.

"Let no one despise your youth." 1 Timothy 4:12

Be louder in prayer than gossip.

Be Bolder in truth than in opinion.

Be braver in worship than in fear.

Be real. Be raw. Be rooted in the Word of God.

Because this world doesn't need more trendy voices.

It needs young prophets.

When it Gets Heavy, Don't Run. Kneel.

When the fight gets hard (and it will)

When temptation knocks (and it will)

When you feel alone (and you might)

Don't run to the world.

Run to the cross.

There is still healing in the name of Jesus. There is still power in His blood. There is still fire in the secret place.

Fall in love with His presence.

Fall in love with holiness.

Fall in love with the mission, to bring Heaven to Earth.

We are Cheering You On

The generation before you? We are not perfect. Gen Z trust me is one of the most needing God generations ever.

But we are praying. Watching.

Believing that you will go further than we did.

You will preach with more fire.

You will stand with more boldness.

You will carry revival deeper into the culture than we could imagine.

Just promise you won't waste it.

Don't waste the time, the gift, the calling, or the fire God has placed in you.

Let it burn. Let it blaze. And let it shake the gates of hell.

"*The people who know their God shall be strong and do great exploits.*" Daniel 11:32

Trust me my generation, your generation and the following generations has potential to have the greatest fire and revival of history. We have college campuses filled with revivals, young adults preaching and bringing people on the street to Christ. We have the resources; we just need to use them.

Final Reflection

Look back on the pages of this book. The hard truths, the battles, the chains, the healing, the call to stand, the name of Jesus, the invitation to burn...

None of it was just for head knowledge. It was a summons to war. A call to rise.

The world is dark, but the darker the night, the brighter the fire. And God didn't put you in this generation by accident. He knew this hour would need your voice.

Now the torch is in your hands.

Journal Prompt:

Spend 10 minutes writing a letter to your future self, or the next generation after you. Tell them what you fight through. What God saved you from. What you want them to carry forward. Seal it with a promise to never let the fire go out.

Prayer:

Jesus, let this fire burn in me until the day I see you face to face. Use my life to awaken a generation and bring revival to a world desperate for you.

About the author

C aleb A. Calloway is a fifteen year old from Cleveland, Ohio, and a committed Christian since the age of eight.

Drawing from his own journey through struggles with lust, depression, suicidal thoughts, and attempts, and family challenges, Caleb writes with raw honest and bold faith. *A Teenage War* is the powerful, authentic book he has long dreamed of writing, born from years of reflection and courage. Caleb believes the only way this generation will change is if young people step up and fight for truth, purity, and hope.

www.ingramcontent.com/pod-product-compliance
Lightning Source LLC
Chambersburg PA
CBHW061831040426
42447CB00012B/2924